CHARLES OLSON AND EDWARD DAHLBERG:
A PORTRAIT OF A FRIENDSHIP

In a photograph that captures many of the textures of their friendship, Dahlberg sits on the left and Olson on the right. (Published with kind permission of the Literary Archives, University of Connecticut Library.)

JOHN CECH

Charles Olson and Edward Dahlberg: A Portrait of a Friendship

ELS
EDITIONS

ELS Editions
Department of English
University of Victoria
Victoria, BC
Canada V8W 3W1
www.elseditions.com

Founding Editor: Samuel L. Macey

General Editor: Luke Carson

Printed by CreateSpace

English literary studies monograph series
ISSN 0829-7681 ; 27
ISBN-10 0-920604-07-2
ISBN-13 978-0-920604-07-6

CONTENTS

PREFACE

In this study of the friendship of Charles Olson and Edward Dahlberg, two of the most interesting figures of modern American letters, I have concentrated on both the human and the artistic dimensions of their contacts with one another—an association which lasted, on and off, for some twenty years. Thus, this portrait is, in part, biographical. I was fortunate enough to have known both writers personally, having attended Olson's last seminar at the University of Connecticut in the fall of 1969 and then meeting Dahlberg a few years later. At the time that Olson was teaching, none of us in his class knew that within a few months he would be dead from cancer, and his untimely death only intensified the profound effects he exerted on most of us who had known and studied with him during those last few, poignant months. I knew then that I would begin a research project involving Olson.

Though I could not prove it at the time, I sensed that there was some strong connection between Olson and Dahlberg. Before encountering Olson, I had become familiar with Dahlberg's work, through his autobiography, *Because I Was Flesh*, and the occasional pieces which he published in places like *The Evergreen Review*. The Beats, rightly or wrongly, had claimed Dahlberg (as they also had Olson) as one of their spiritual and artistic mentors. Dahlberg took enormous chances in his soaring, idiosyncratic prose, and he made fascinating personal voyages in his essays. His volume on American culture and writers, *Do These Bones Live*, was then an underground model (along with William Carlos Williams' *In The American Grain* and D. H. Lawrence's *Studies in Classic American Literature*) for how criticism could be written—forcefully, subjectively, liberated from the restrictions of academic formulas. I knew Dahlberg had influenced Olson's poetry, as Olson noted in his most important theoretical essay, "Projective Verse," but it was not clear to me then how deep or long Olson's learning from Dahlberg had been. What was certain was that they shared a similar source for their stylistic energies and subject matter.

When Olson's papers were purchased by The University of Connecticut Library and the Olson Archives were established there in 1971, all those vague connections and intuitions took on a more solid form. I was able to pore through boxes of Olson's manuscripts and letters and read the marginalia in his personal library. From these sources I discovered that Olson and Dahlberg had known each other quite well. In fact, they had been on close, friendly terms for a number of years in their respective artistic careers. Many of Dahlberg's letters to Olson were among Olson's papers, and I soon located Olson's letters to Dahlberg at the University of Texas, which is the repository for many of Dahlberg's private and literary manuscripts. My research took me to other libraries with other collections of correspondence between Dahlberg and Olson or their mutual friends. These library investigations led to interviews and correspondence with some of those literary figures who had known both Olson and Dahlberg when they were working together.

Finally, I approached Edward Dahlberg, who was then living and writing in New York City, and we visited and later corresponded and talked at great length about his friendship with Olson. In fact, Dahlberg continued to write to me about Olson up until his own death in 1977, though I had finished the first version of this study in 1974. Their fractured friendship still obsessed him, and he could never fully free himself from the injuries he felt he suffered because of Olson. He had his opinions about Olson, but he respected my need to tell both sides of the story, and he gave me blanket permission to quote from his letters, to offer his version in his own words, free of censorship. Without his generosity and his timely and tireless support my work may not have been possible. Indeed, he showed me, as he told me the first time we met, that he "has nothing to hide."

Artistic influences are like a network of tributaries to main streams that flow into the whole of a writer's work. Thus, the matter of identifying these contributing sources has been guided by a personal impulse, urged on by the sheer love of adventure and discovery, and sustained by the admiration I have for both writers. In attempting to fathom some of the mysteries surrounding Olson's and Dahlberg's lives and works, one naturally partakes of the events themselves, and that, in itself, is compelling. I have tried to map this human realm in Olson's and Dahlberg's friendship, in the hope that some of the private matters it has necessarily involved going into will help to cast some light on the lives and art of both men.

My controlling purpose throughout has been to explore the effects their close contacts had on their actions and the works they were producing while they were friends. The study is meant to be taken as a chapter—a small but powerful one—in their careers. I have included sufficient background material (biographical, historical, literary, political) to provide a stage on which the events of their friendship could be re-enacted. I have not attempted an exhaustive analysis of Dahlberg's and Olson's individual work, speculating on how their friendship may have affected the total body of their writing—this would have been a huge and perhaps an impossible task, since many of the effects are intangible and hence not demonstrable. Also, such an undertaking would have blurred the focus of this study. Similarly, I have not sought to recapitulate the much larger context of literary or cultural history of which both men were and are a part. This area of investigation is also vast, and it would take a separate study to justly "set" Olson and Dahlberg in their literary times.

Ultimately, however, I have refrained from these amplifications because I have not wished to be repetitive, since a number of studies have appeared in recent years which speak to these wider concerns about Olson and Dahlberg. I would therefore suggest that the reader of this study seek out such works as Charles DeFanti's excellent biography of Dahlberg, *The Wages of Expectation*; Charles Boer's moving memoir of Olson, *Charles Olson in Connecticut*; Sherman Paul's fine "setting" of Olson in *Olson's Push: Origin, Black Mountain and Recent American Poetry*; and George Butterick's thoroughly engrossing and meticulous commentary on Olson's life and writing in his *Guide to the Maximus Poems* and in the ten issues of *Olson*, the journal based on the unpublished manuscripts in the Olson Archives at Connecticut. These are only a few of the studies which serve to indicate the growing awareness of the importance of Olson and Dahlberg in modern American letters.

In the end, I hope that this study may return the reader to the works of Olson and Dahlberg—especially to Dahlberg. His writings have never drawn the following that Olson's have, though Dahlberg's work is equally bold and provocative and of particular interest to anyone concerned with mythic approaches to American culture and its literature. Despite all of Dahlberg's warnings and protestations about the American writer's compulsion to be unique and original, he remains one of the most singular voices of our contemporary literature. Paul Carroll has said: "in Edward Dahlberg we have a classic on our own back porch. One reads him at one's peril. At its best his prose asks nothing less than Cardinal Newman's motto: *cor ad cor loquitor*, 'heart speaketh to heart.'"

In the preparation of this study, I wish to acknowledge and thank several university libraries for so generously making the materials in their holdings available to me. They are: The University of Pennsylvania Library and its Special Collections, which include Waldo Frank's papers and Dahlberg's letters to Frank; The Collection of American Literature at the Bienecke Rare Book and Manuscript Library at Yale University for allowing me access to and permission to quote from Dahlberg's letters to Alfred Stieglitz, Dudley Nichols, and Dorothy Norman; The Humanities Research Center of the University of Texas Library in Austin for permission to quote from the Olson letters to Dahlberg.

Unpublished material by Charles Olson from among his papers in the Literary Archives, University of Connecticut Library, is copyright by the University of Connecticut and used here with the Library's permission. Other unpublished material by Charles Olson, including excerpts from his letters to Edward Dahlberg and Dorothy Norman, is copyright by the Estate of Charles Olson, and is likewise used here by permission. The Estate of Edward Dahlberg retains the copyright on the unpublished Dahlberg material, including his letters to Olson and others, which are quoted here with the Estate's permission. My deep gratitude to both Estates and the Literary Archives at Connecticut for granting me permission to quote from the unpublished writings of both authors.

Personally, I wish to offer my heartfelt thanks to the following individuals for their invaluable help in the completion of this study: to Dorothy Norman, for graciously clarifying the *Twice-A-Year* sections of this study and for allowing me to quote from her private papers among the holdings of the Bienecke at Yale; to Charles DeFanti, for providing me with invaluable biographical information about Dahlberg's career, for his many thoughtful letters, for his steady encouragement, and for his friendship; to Harold Billings for his wisdom and insightful critical suggestions throughout the development of this study; to George Butterick and Charles Boer who saw the manuscript through its birth pains with patient care; to Sherman Paul, for reminding me about that fabled blue pencil and for guiding it through the revisions; and, finally to my dear friend, Hernan Vera, who saw to it that the manuscript was kept, "in circulation."

There is one other who here should be given special credit—my wife, Eve. I dedicate this study to her, with my abiding love. She endured the gestation, the writing, and the completion of this work with me and has remained through it all my most loving critic.

Cambridge, Massachusetts, 1974
Gainesville, Florida, 1981

CHAPTER ONE

Beginnings

... so apart and incommunicable have been our own poets that we search for letters, for buried momentoes and fragments of conversations to disclose whether Herman Melville perchance had even heard of *Leaves of Grass*, whether Poe and Melville had met or whether *Moby-Dick* was known at all to the celestially pulse-less Brahmins.—EDWARD DAHLBERG, *Do These Bones Live*

Edward Dahlberg and Charles Olson first met on a Sunday evening, August 9, 1936. Dahlberg was spending the summer in Gloucester, Massachusetts, taking his annual retreat from the heat and pace of New York City in order to begin work on his first book of essays dealing with American culture and literature. Olson was finishing up the month as a substitute letter-carrier in Gloucester. In the fall he planned to go to Harvard to begin doctoral work there as one of the first students in the new History of American Civilization program. Their meeting would tie them together for the next twenty years.

"We met by the merest chance," Dahlberg wrote his friend, the photographer Alfred Stieglitz. "He happened to hear of me through a tweedle-dee-tweedlum professor at City College who mentioned in the course of conversation that I was a little acid about Mumford's work."[1] Olson had known about Dahlberg prior to the unidentified professor's remark. He had read Dahlberg's first novel, *Bottom Dogs*. But the fact that Dahlberg showed interest in Herman Melville no doubt whetted Olson's curiosity and precipitated their meeting. Melville had been Olson's subject in his Master's Thesis at Wesleyan University in 1933.[2] In 1934 Olson located Melville's long missing, personal library, thus opening an important new dimension in Melville scholarship. Part of Olson's reason for going to Harvard was to continue his research on Melville under the direction of F. O. Matthiessen. Ultimately, though, he wished to do his own study of Melville. In a very real sense, then, Melville caused Dahlberg's and Olson's meeting and catalyzed their friendship.

Dahlberg remembered an odd, coincidental circumstance of that first encounter with Olson for this writer;[3] the off-key, upright piano in the parlour of the boarding house on Mt. Pleasant Avenue had begun to play when

Olson knocked on the door. This small detail serves as an ironic foreshadowing of the discordant notes that would later be struck in their friendship. Dahlberg recalled other details in a letter to Harold Billings:

> Two quack painters, and are there any other kind today, used to have Sunday evenings; after singing hymns, they passed out their canvases, and expected those who came to purchase them. I could not tolerate these pimps of the arts, and never attended the Sunday evening affairs. On one of those nights a young man named Charles Olson arrived, and he asked to see me, but I declined, and remained in my room cloistered away from all these fools. It was about 8 or so when he arrived; by midnight a man knocked at my door, and announced the man was still waiting to see me. I felt very ashamed and went down stairs, and saw this giant. We talked for two and a half hours; he was then an adherent of Twain and Melville. He expressed unlimited admiration for my work, then quite barbaric, and as I never knew how to handle people shrewdly, he soon became my friend.[4]

Dahlberg's other remarks also ring with some retrospective irony, in light of the later strained relations between the two. However, at the time there was nothing off-key about Dahlberg's feelings for Olson: he was extremely impressed. He wrote to Stieglitz soon after their meeting to announce his discovery. He told Stieglitz that Olson was "one of those porous personalities who, I believe, will do something with his life."[5] And it is with something close to wonder that he continued to marvel at Olson's enthusiasm, articulateness, and remarkable memory.[6]

Their first converastion concerned Melville and Shakespeare. Olson had discovered Shakespeare's inspiration in Melville's shaping of *Moby-Dick* when he located Melville's seven-volume edition of Shakespeare and deciphered Melville's short-hand marginalia. The significance of Olson's discovery was a revelation to Dahlberg. Dahlberg was fascinated by Melville's return to a master of the past to guide him in his creation. Dahlberg's own criticism of American literature had not yet germinated into a comprehensive vision, but later he would say that he detested contemporary American fiction, precisely because it failed to graft itself on to a larger literary tradition, and he would write Stieglitz repeatedly on this point. Certainly the connection between Melville and Shakespeare Olson introduced him to was a telling piece of evidence that he would later synthesize in the general conception of *Do These Bones Live*, the book that matured during their first four years of friendship. Very simply, the idea of the book was an extended exhortation of the American writer to quit his obsession with originality and instead to acknowledge and learn to work within the tradition of world literature of which he could not help but be a part.

Later in August, after they had spent more time together, Dahlberg again wrote Stieglitz about Olson, this time showing concern for Olson's welfare:

Olson improves with time; he is going up to Harvard to teach this Fall and doesn't like it all; but I should hate to see him get in difficulties there and not know where to turn for his bread and butter. So I am going to caution him, not to be deeply cautious, but not to permit unimportant details of drab-tasting every day life to impinge on him—something I have never succeeded in doing, which has been most unfortunate with me.[7]

In his "Journal, begun Sept. 1, 1936,"[8] Olson offered some indication of the effects of his first exchanges with Dahlberg. He jots down a number of books and authors ("Bourne/Beara/Lenin/Gorki/Marx/O'Niel, James/A. M. Simons, Social Forces in America") prefacing the list with the heading: "to reduce my socio-politico-economic naivete." Later in the same journal, Olson goes on to note that

Dahlberg nudges:
1. Laocoon
2. Frazer
3. Frank, Waldo
    America Hispana
    Rediscovery of Am.
4. Harrison, Jane
    Ancient Art & Ritual
Migel de Unamuno
        Tragic sense of Life
        The soliloquies & Conversations of Don Quixote

This new data serves as a buoy, marking the channel of the friendship that had begun to form between the two men. Interestingly, one of the few notes Olson recorded after his first visits with Dahlberg was a booklist. This kind of exchange of intellectual resources would continue throughout their friendship. The fact that their first encounters struck this note of interchange of books and ideas was especially important, since both men were at turning points in their respective lives.

*　*　*

By the spring of 1936 Dahlberg had stopped writing novels. He turned instead toward a critique of what he called the "contemporary mess" of American fiction. He objected to the writing of most of his contemporaries (including Hemingway, Dos Passos, Faulkner, Farrell); and the vehemence he intended to direct at the current new wave of fiction writers included an equally bitter disavowal of his own novels, particularly of their style. The spring of 1936 found Dahlberg completely disenchanted "with the tone and direction of his own writing."[9]

That tone had been starkly realistic in his first three novels (*Bottom Dogs* (1929); *From Flushing to Calvary* (1932); and *Those Who Perish* (1934)) where his direction had been shaped by the need to express the futility "of the dollarless American trapped in a capitalistic society."[10] D. H. Lawrence had agreed to contribute what ended up being an ambiguous introduction to the first novel, *Bottom Dogs*. While praising the book's honesty, Lawrence felt the characters and events to be so "offensive" as to be just this side of "legal insanity." Though he said he was "glad" to have read the book, Lawrence was also happy to have finished with Dahlberg's "last word in repulsive consciousness, consciousness in a state of repulsion."[11]

Many of the events of *Bottom Dogs* had sprung directly from Dahlberg's own troubled youth. The autobiographical thread would weave itself through the other novels until, in two later books, *Because I was Flesh* (1961) and *The Confessions of Edward Dahlberg* (1971), Dahlberg cast aside the purely fictional mode and instead attempted to come to terms directly with the traumatic facts of his life. At all points, though, the record of Dahlberg's experiences as a boy and young man appear to be a bleak and desperate terrain of disturbing circumstances, a personal mythos which he could never fully exhaust or exorcise. In her able analysis of Dahlberg's work, Josephine Herbst maintains that the recurrent autobiographical note in Dahlberg's writing expressed his "compulsive willingness to pick at the same themes and characters, over and over, which is the mark of a profound but fertile uncertainty. It is the kind of uncertainty ... which was to compel Dahlberg to submit his experiences to revisions and, finally, to a long submersion in the dark, before they could emerge in the perfected meanings of *Because I was Flesh*."[12]

For Dahlberg, *Bottom Dogs* began the journey back to his origins. Like the novel's main character, Dahlberg was born in Boston in 1900, and like the book's hero, he was the illegitimate son of a lady barber. Dahlberg's mother's name was Elizabeth Dalberg—Dahlberg later added the extra letter to the name, thinking it gave it a more cosmopolitan Swedish sound. Jonathan Williams summarizes:

> The book is a series of vignettes. It begins in Kansas City in the Teddy Roosevelt era and concerns Lizzie Lewis, a lady barber, and her young son Lorrie. Lizzie had run off from her husband, a fur operator in Brooklyn, with a barber years ago. He turned out to be a chippie-chaser and a pimp, so she ducked him in Dallas, Denver, Memphis, etc., and landed in K.C. Lizzie takes up with a river man, "Kentucky Blue Grass Henry

14

Smith," who wants Lorrie out of the way. Lorrie [Edward] is dispatched [by Lizzie] to an orphanage in Cleveland.[13]

So far all the scenes of the book were drawn from life. His unfortunate mother had shipped him off to the Jewish Orphan Asylum in Cleveland when he was eleven, so that she could have a better chance of landing a marriage proposal from one of her numerous "suitors." Dahlberg's descriptions of the orphanage in the novel were what struck Lawrence "with amazement [at] how rapidly the human psyche can strip itself of its awareness and its emotional contacts, and reduce itself to a subbrutal condition of simple gross persistence. It is not animality—far from it. These boys are much less than animals. They are cold wills functioning with a minimum of consciousness. . . . They have no hopes, no desires even. They have even no will-to-exist, for existence even is too high a term."[14]

After release from the orphanage at 17, Dahlberg, like the novel's main character, Lorrie Lewis, returned to Kansas City. As in the novel, Dahlberg spent the rest of his late teens "on the bum," riding the rails, feeding himself when and however he could, working at the most menial and demeaning of jobs. In essence, the years were cruel, vagrant, aimless, leading him

to Salt Lake City, Portland, Frisco, and into L.A., where he takes up residence at the Y.M.C.A. Again, there is a lot of acuity in this writing. It is sharp and mordant; he is writing about a sleazy down-and-out world and doing it with gusto. . . . *Bottom Dogs* ends in Solomon's Dancepalace. Lorrie sees an hallucinatory vision of the City—"God, he hadn't really known he had been up against all that. . . . Perhaps, he would go east, get out of it all, he could run away; but he couldn't go side-door Pullman again, that was finished. Boing, sleeping in coal cars, riding those railroad broncos, going to strange hotel rooms, the ghastly plaster inside those empty clothes-closets, walking the streets—all that was done, but then, how did he know? Anyhow, if he got the clap he would go to the Los Angeles City Hospital; maybe, those enamelled iron beds, the sheets, the medical immaculateness of it all, might do something to him. Something had to happen; and he knew nothing would. . . ."[15]

The novel ends elliptically, inconclusively with the passage quoted by Williams above.

Lawrence may have objected to the book, calling it a "*ne plus ultra*" of defeat. However, its bleak portrayal of the underdog side of the American experience earned Dahlberg a reputation as a proletarian novelist. Dahlberg had met and known Lawrence briefly in England in the late 1920's. Lawrence's parting advice to him had been: "Try not to be unlucky, and always write with a great bitterness."[16] Dahlberg took the advice. With some of the worst years of the Depression setting in, *Bottom Dogs* and the two other

15

novels that quickly followed attracted acclaim and interest from those involved in social and economic reform. As Harold Billings put it: "Those early 1930's were restless, political years for the writer as everyone else, and Dahlberg's proletarian canticles were generally welcomed among the socialist literati as were the works of any author who touched on the tragedy of human existence."[17]

The second novel, *From Flushing to Calvary* (1932) continued the story of Lorrie and Lizzie. If anything, the portrait of their collective misfortunes is painted here in even starker tones than in *Bottom Dogs*. The scene changes to New York City during the Depression. Lorrie picks up odd jobs and barely manages to eke out an existence. Lizzie, more impoverished and in failing health, joins him there. They take a cold water flat facing a cemetery in Bensonhurst, Queens. (The reappearance of Lizzie in the second novel was a fictional addition. Dahlberg's mother had remained in Kansas City, suffering through several major operations.) In the novel, Lizzie sets herself up as a health advisor and dispenser of herbal medicines to the other denizens of the tenement and the neighborhood. Her methods, however, are sheer quackery, and one of her specialties (trying to induce abortions by a nauseating Indian potion) nearly gets her into trouble with the law. There is a harrowing episode when she is caught shoplifting a cheap necklace from a 5 & 10¢ store and is bullied by the store detective. Finally she dies, alone in the flat, and an absent Lorrie finds her decomposing body in the grimy bedroom a few days later.

Dazed, Lorris wanders back into Manhattan, eventually to Greenwich Village, where he is swept up in a Communist worker's demonstration and clubbed to the pavement when the police break the ranks of the marchers. Throughout, Lorrie is presented as a withdrawn, bookish young man—unskilled, unenlightened, and finally unable to connect his beating with the political events that have caused it. All he can remember is a hymn he was taught at the orphanage. Singing the song while the blood congeals on his wound, he limps away from the melee and the novel ends. Again he is choiceless, his actions are inconclusive. He simply loses himself in the crowd.

Dahlberg recalled in *The Confessions* that *From Flushing to Calvary* was branded as "defeatist" by the "socialist literati."[18] But in an essay shortly after the book was published, he defended his artistic choices, his characters, and the milieu he describes in the novel:

> Of course, it is true that all the bottom dog drifters ... are ineluctably doomed at the outset of the novel. But no matter what one may charge this gelatinous mass of floating population with, it is certainly inaccurate to lay defeatism upon their backs also, because that implies a choice, which

they have never had, simply because they never knew they had one. For one of the very few reasons that they don't take their hunger and social abasement singing the *Internationale* is that they have never heard of it. Never heard of Communism. Words like *Bolshevism* either do not exist in their vocabulary at all, or are at best a kind of obscenity to be included in the national lavatory esoterica.... Now in order to please the Communists I might have had Lorrie dash up to the *New Masses* offices or elsewhere and ask for membership in the Party. But then I would no longer be a novelist but a liar.[19]

In October of 1932 at the time of *From Flushing to Calvary*'s publication, Dahlberg was still in strong sympathy with the causes of the Left. Though never a Party member himself, Dahlberg was an active spokesman and writer for social change. Yet already a split was developing between Dahlberg's personal aims as an artist and the ideological expectations he felt his associates on the Left were asking him to fulfill. By 1936, when he met Olson, his connections with the Left were almost completely severed and he had bitterly reacted against the imposition of any Party bias on his work. As early as 1932, he felt that his interest as an artist lay in portraying human problems. And he began early to assert fiercely his literary independence.

Unlike his bottom-dog characters Dahlberg had not gone unschooled or totally deprived. Dahlberg had hoboed to the West Coast, having survived the emotional horrors of an orphanage. Certainly this was a powerful and disruptive experience in his childhood. However, the orphanage years had not been quite so demeaning and sterile as he made them out to be in *Bottom Dogs*.[20] Nevertheless, he was "starved for affection" and consequently withdrew into books. The result was that he "fell completely in love with English" during the orphanage years. In California, after several years of working, reading, a few unpublished attempts at writing, and even a brief stint as a script writer for a Hollywood studio,[21] he enrolled as a student of philosophy at Berkeley.

Dahlberg published several stories in the University's literary magazine, *The Occident*, which he later referred to as juvenile "hemorrhages of melancholy." After two years at Berkeley, he transferred to Columbia, where he took his Bachelor's degree in Philosophy in 1925. After teching briefly in a New York City public high school, he went to Europe where he began to work on *Bottom Dogs* in 1927. There he met Hart Crane, D. H. Lawrence, and the group of artists and writers clustered around Ethel Moorehead in Monte Carlo. He contributed a number of works to her journal, *This Quarter*—among these were portions of *Bottom Dogs*, several poems, and an essay, "Ariel in Caliban."[22] In the essay Dahlberg acknowledged his debt to Joyce and particularly to *A Portrait of the Artist as a Young Man* for

17

the creative and semi-autobiographical impulse that was, at the time, guiding him in *Bottom Dogs*.

Despite the connections he was making, the two years in Europe were exhausting. He returned to America, just as *Bottom Dogs* was released in this country and the stock market coincidentally crashed. The subsequent attention the book received was not solely confined to political quarters. In recognition of his promise as a writer, Dahlberg was invited to work on his second novel at the MacDowell Artist's Colony in Peterborough, New Hampshire. With the appearance of *From Flushing to Calvary*, he was asked to contribute fiction and to report on political affairs for journals of some prominence, including *Pagany*, *The New Republic*, *The Nation*, and *New Masses*.

In 1933 he travelled to Europe again, perhaps because of a writing commission to do a travel article on a particular steamship line, perhaps as a freelance journalist.[23] Whatever the reasons for his going, he came away from Germany, a few months later, certain that Hitler was to be taken at his word. A beating he received in Berlin at the hands of one of the Hitler Youth had removed whatever doubts he may have had.[24] The sense of impending catastrophe for the world, and the Jews in particular, fed the pessimistic outlook of his third novel, *Those Who Perish*, published in 1934. Essentially, the story involves American Jews who are too apathetic to understand the seriousness of Hitler's anti-Semitic threat and blandly go about their business. Few people in New Republic, Dahlberg's fictional borough of New York City, believe the German propaganda or the rumors of Nazi atrocities already beginning to whisper their way out of Germany. But the anti-Semitism abroad in the world is brought home when gangs of American brownshirts begin to harass the neighborhood. The only two characters who are sensitive to the corrupt life of the community end up dead by the novel's end—one through suicide and the other through starvation. The book closes ominously, with an apocalyptic sunset, the sky torn by barbed wire, suggestive of the holocaust that was to come.

Once more Dahlberg's novelistic concerns and sympathies are with the little people, those whose lives are extinguished by the passive and pitiless order of things, whether Hitler's tyranny or the more subtle prejudices of the wealthy Jewish leaders of the community center. But the message of the book is not a political one. Rather it is prophetic. Dahlberg is here suggesting that if compassion fails, if human needs are debased or ignored, the result is death, either in the microcosm of the Jewish community in the Bronx or in the larger arena of world affairs. In this, his third novel, Dahlberg felt he was beginning to "rid [himself] of scatophagous naturalism"[25] in order to truthfully portray the sorry condition of life he witnessed. The experience in the Jewish community had also been partially his own, for he had been briefly connected in 1931 with the Jewish Community Center in Jersey City.

Dahlberg recalls in *The Confessions* that this novel was also disapproved of by his Marxist confreres. Dahlberg has continued to insist that his failure to conform to the party's literary standards forced this book into limbo with the other two. In order to help promote the book and to make an ally he introduced himself to Waldo Frank, a leading figure of the writers on the Left, an editor for *The New Republic*, and later Dahlberg's friend:

> I mailed you my latest and third novel, *Those Who Perish*, almost two weeks ago. I wonder if you have read it and whether you are favorably disposed toward it. I want to make an appeal to you. The reason is as follows: My book is being noiselessly lowered in a casket. While the Trail of Fu Manchu and fiction about Three Young Ladies are being vulgarly bugled, my novel is being committed to a still-born birth. Books are sold out in the same way that strikes are and for the same reasons. . . . and the simplest way to annihilate such a book is not to write about it at all.
>
> While . . . the New York Times sheds cellophane tears over the press and the state of civil rights in the Soviet Union . . . [it] has been exercising a censorship on books with a class-bias worthy of a Goebbels. I think the time is ripe for a collective writers' protest against these dollar columnists of the daily press. If you beleive that my book warrants a serious hearing by readers, I would be grateful to you if you would say so.[26]

Frank was sympathetic to Dahlberg's plight and wrote a jacket-liner note for the novel. The book was favorably reviewed by Kenneth Burke in *The New Republic*. But by 1937 it had sold only 200 copies. The meager sales of the other books, along with the running verbal debate on the political efficacy of his novels, led Dahlberg to conclude that his talents were being deliberately ignored and stifled.

However, around the time of *Those Who Perish* Dahlberg had not yet given up the fight for social change and was still politically active. In 1935 he helped organize the American Writer's Congress, an anti-Fascist organization including as members distinguished writers such as Van Wyck Brooks, Kenneth Burke, Lewis Mumford, Clifford Odets, Nelson Algren, and Richard Wright. The minutes of a colloquium held at the first Writer's Congress reveal Dahlberg's concerns at this moment in his career. His remarks are telling because of their emphasis on the importance Dahlberg was already beginning to place on a shared, emotional tradition in all writing:

> The last participant in the discussion was Edward Dahlberg, who declared that the revolutionary movement must "build up our writers." He declared that the neglect of them in the bourgeois literary media must not be

19

duplicated in the revolutionary press. "What has really happened," he said, "is that the person who engages in controversies and in critical discussions is immediately charged with having a personal animus against this or that person, simply because he passionately believes in literature and wants to build up a literature. You can not build up a literature without passion, and if you have no passion you had better stop writing altogether."[27]

In the margin of a letter to Waldo Frank during the same year Dahlberg extended his argument to include the roles of criticism and the critic: "I believe that criticism that does not bear the marks of violent collision with the original sources is just passive scenario writing at the best."[28]

During the same conference Dahlberg "collided" with the works of Hemingway, Dos Passos, and Erskine Caldwell. He recalled in *The Confessions* the attack he had made on their work: he detested their naturalism and resented their reduction of "the old traditional style of feeling embodied in such words as morals, good, evil, honesty, kindness, pity, and principles"[29] to "a gallimaufry of ferine neologisms and a drabbish language."[30] He was heckled by a Party-serving garment worker in the audience who rebuked his attack on Hemingway and Dos Passos, to which Dahlberg retorted, "Comrade, you ply your needle and I'll take care of literature."[31]

By the mid-1930's, the conflict between Dahlberg's own artistic values and the ideology he was being asked to support had moved into the open. Dahlberg was incensed by the use the Left made of writers who were beginning to gain some popularity and thus be of use to the movement. He loathed the promotional cocktail parties designed to inflate reputations. Most of all, he resented the fact that his own work had received such slim support. Harold Billings, the curator of Dahlberg's papers at The University of Texas and Dahlberg's long-time friend, adds another element to the understanding of Dahlberg's mounting disillusionment with the Left: "Dahlberg has always been a wild, mustang spirit and fettered only by moral corrals, not by social or political movements. It was only natural that he should become estranged from Marxism, and a mutual bitterness still exists between him and many former fellow-travellers."[32] For Dahlberg, the Communists' hypocritical exploitation of workers and artists was ultimately as abhorent as capitalistic injustice.

Like so many others he had envisioned Communism in human terms. He asks himself in *The Confessions*:

> Why did I become a Communist? All just men covet a utopia.... The intelligentsia of America were powerfully stung by the sufferings of the humble people. The richest nation on earth was afflicted with an artificial

20

famine that bankrupted the shopkeepers and was at the same time a benison to industrialists who hoarded an immense store of gold, properties and land.

The poor were unlike dogs who could paw the ground and dig up bones that had been hid and saved against the day of hunger. The corporate farms were not choked with tares, but were overladen with wheat, barley, and the pastures were pestered with millions upon millions of kine, sheep and porkers.[33]

But Dahlberg could not restrain his disdain for the manipulations of the Left. He had seen enough of the Party infighting to know that he could not morally condone its maneuvering. He believed that the revolution, if it came, would be horribly bloody and only lead to ultimate reaction.

Though he had published quite a few reviews and articles between 1929 and 1934, they had, from his point of view, brought him little in return. His application for a Guggenheim in 1935 was refused. Though his fortunes were at a low ebb, Dahlberg did not contemplate abandoning writing; he accepted the risks and sacrifices. In a letter to Allen Tate in 1962, he sketched with some self-mockery his choice of vocation: "I know I made many craven errors, and I resolved as early as '34 to be a man of letters, and to be an eremite to do so.... now at the age of sixty-two, I am still learning how to compose one sentence, and if I am unusually lucky I may be able to do it."[34]

Josephine Herbst called Dahlberg's period as a novelist a "captivity" rooted in "his own constricted consciousness" and the "temporal chaos" of the events Dahlberg tried to confront as a political activist.[35] He tried to start another novel, *Bitch Goddess*, early in 1936. A part of the book appeared in *Signature*, a small journal, but Dahlberg soon lost interest in this "Notes to a novel in progress," as it was called in the magazine. It was an oppressive time. Dahlberg wrote Stieglitz to confess that he "did not know where 'tin can' realism left off and where what was profoundly living and significant began."[36]

The ceiling had fallen in, quite literally, on Dahlberg's affairs in New York. An enormous chunk of plaster worked itself loose from the ceiling and collapsed his bed one afternoon while he was out for a walk. Within a few days Dahlberg left New York for Gloucester in what Herbst interprets as a "deliberate absence from the obligations and expectations of the active world he aimed to master by retreat" and to find "a stillness in which the voices of the oracles may be heard."[37] More practically, the vacation allowed Dahlberg to start work on the "small volume" on contemporary American writing he had mentioned to Stieglitz. Originally, Dahlberg's intent was to attack contemporary American fiction, including his own first two novels. After meeting Olson, though, the project soon expanded.

According to his and others' accounts, Dahlberg had undergone a painful and finally limiting phase of growth as a writer in the seven years since *Bottom Dogs* had appeared. Olson's energy and enthusiasm undoubtedly refreshed him after the frustrations of New York. Dahlberg wrote Stieglitz that there was much he could do to help guide Olson through the politics and pitfalls of writing. Dahlberg readily sympathized with his younger visitor, who was in his own state of crisis.

* * *

Ten years younger than Dahlberg, Charles Olson had been born into a kinder world. In contrast to Dahlberg's painful childhood, Olson's earliest memories are happy ones, of growing up in Worcester, Massachusetts, and of having a normal family life. An only child, Olson was very close to both of his parents, but particularly to his father, Karl, who was a shaping force in Olson's boyhood. What impressed Olson most about his father was his deep and honest engagement in everything he did: his mail route, his correspondence art courses, his piano playing, practical joking, mending of the kitchen sink, or fervent discourses on American history. According to Olson, Karl did nothing half-heartedly; and he passed on to his son this gift of being able to be totally immersed in one's work: "the satisfaction of a job lay in the doing of it."[38]

Karl Olson, a Swedish immigrant, attached great significance to the history and possibilities of his new country. A democratic sense of fair-play led him to become an early union organizer among the letter-carriers and to courageously engage the postal administration in a bitter fight for better working conditions and benefits. The strain of this ordeal, Olson later recalled in his memoir of his father, "The Post Office," resulted in Karl's sudden death in 1935 of a cerebral hemorrhage, just as he was anticipating a victory in the union's negotiations. "The Post Office" is an act of homage on Olson's part to his father's strength and dignity. Karl was an uncompromising individual, unfortunately pitted against a governmental bureaucracy that grew more impersonal and vindictive with the later years of his service. Karl's death, about a year after Olson's completion of his M.A. at Wesleyan was perhaps the only tragic shadow in Olson's otherwise happy boyhood and youth. Olson and his father had quarreled just before Karl's death. The argument had not been settled, and the guilt that Olson attached to the incident clawed at him into the next summer at the time he met Dahlberg.

Olson's mother, Mary, had been and remained the stable center of Olson's life. She provided him with his religious education—Roman Catholic (though neither Olson nor his father were faithful church-goers). She rescued him from his father's rare spankings. She was somewhat moody (as Olson remembered in a poem, "While the Dead Prey Upon Us," written many years later), and in terms of energy she was the antithesis of both her son and her husband. Together the two parents willingly sacrificed their comfort for the success of their only child. While Dahlberg's childhood had been bleak and unpromising, Olson's was sheltered and warm.

Olson blossomed at Worcester's Classical High School. There he was captain of the "Declamation Team" and student council president in his junior year. In his final year (1927) he was Senior Class President, an honor student, and finished third in the National Oratorical Contest, winning a trip to Europe during the summer of 1928. His high school yearbook, *Classic Myths*, described him as: "Gifted with a charming personality, a sterling character and a keen mind, Charles has easily assumed the leadership of our class. A model student, he has guided successfully the Student Council and the Debating Assembly, where he has made a host of friends."[39]

In the fall of 1928 Olson enrolled at Wesleyan University in Middletown, Connecticut. Once again, his academic performance drew honors: he was Phi Beta Kappa, one of the school's champion debaters, the editorialist for the college newspaper, and class historian at commencement. Upon his graduation in 1932, his literature teacher and advisor Wilbert Snow, influenced Olson in his decision to continue at Wesleyan in the graduate program in English. It was at about this time that Olson, again through Snow, became thoroughly engrossed in the work of Herman Melville.

Snow recalled:

> When Charles Olson was at Wesleyan he asked me if I would direct him while he wrote a treatise on Melville as an M.A. thesis. I told him I would, but only on one condition—that he agree not to read what other people had written about Melville. He consented and we went through all of Melville's prose chronologically. It was a monumental task but Charlie was equal to it. The thesis was his own original estimate of the man and his work and it won him a Master's degree.[40]

He went on to provide a more personal view of Olson, as he knew him at Wesleyan. The impression, subjective as it may be, helps to give a sense of the imprint Olson invariably left on those who worked closely with him:

> Few students ever made on me the impact that Charlie Olson did. He was an original thinker, a stutterer to the stars, and an endless dreamer. I knew him first as a debater when I coached the debating teams of the college. With his height of six feet eight inches, and his booming voice,

23

he was so overpowering on the platform that the judges didn't dare give the decision to anybody else! . . . I urged him to give his life to politics and government. I told him people needed his power, his oratory, his clear thinking, that the greatest lack in politics in America is that politicians don't have imagination—which Charlie did have. But no. He wanted to be a poet first of all.[41]

The poetry came much later, but only after Olson, ironically, had served a brief and rather disillusioning stint in politics.

Olson's interest in Melville had begun in the summers in the seaport town of Gloucester. Olson's father was attracted to the sea and the excitement of a vital tradition still in process in the fishing industry of the busy town. From his early teens, Olson spent most of his summers there. He and his father kept extensive scrapbooks of newspaper clippings about Gloucester's heritage and the exploits of the fishermen. To deepen his son's understanding of the fishing industry's history, Karl gave Olson his first copy of *Moby-Dick* when he was seventeen.

Olson's master's thesis presented a textual study of the whole of Melville's fiction and provided the first complete bibliography of Melville's publications and Melville criticism, though Snow had insisted that Olson stay away from the criticism until he had settled on his own ideas about Melville. Beyond this, one of Olson's main concerns was to construct a biographical "portrait" of Melville's youth and early days as a sailor. Olson sought the psychological links between these formative experiences and the author's later works, especially *Moby-Dick*. He tried to account for Melville's "fascination with suffering and death. . . . the damnable injustice of it all, Melville could never get out of his mind . . . the mainspring of his criticism of life, this ungodly incongruity."[42] Thus, early on in his work on Melville, Olson's attentions were directed to Melville's tormented personal and psychic life. This same emphasis later provided much of the uniqueness of *Call Me Ishmael*, the study about Melville Olson eventually published in 1947. Already, though, the M.A. thesis struggled to reveal the darker side of Melville's creative personality. In his thesis Olson also focused on Melville's reading and the possible effects it may have had on him at various points in his career. Olson speculated on the strong influence of the Elizabethans in the stylistic energy Melville displayed in *Moby-Dick*, and Olson drew the analogy between Lear and Ahab, even before he had unearthed Melville's volumes of Shakespeare, which made the claim a fact.

After completing the thesis in the spring of 1933, Olson was able to continue his research with the financial assistance of an Olin Fellowship that Snow helped him to secure. In the winter of 1934, through Melville's granddaughter, Eleanor Melville Metcalf, Olson succeeded in uncovering the ninety-five volumes from Melville's personal library, including his collection of Hawthorne and his heavily annotated, seven-volume edition of Shakespeare. The intuitions of the M.A. thesis proved true. Shakespeare was of central importance to Melville in the composition of *Moby-Dick*.

The bringing to light of the library has become one of the most important contributions to Melville scholarship—equalled only, as Ann Charters points out, by Raymond Weaver's discovery of the manuscript for *Billy* Budd in 1919. Mrs. Metcalf's confidence in Olson gained him access to the Melville family papers. These private documents turned out to be as important a find for Olson as the library because of their revelations about the personal lives of Melville, his family, and his friends.[43]

Olson proceeded to decipher Melville's marginalia that appeared throughout his books. As shall be seen later, the most dramatic findings came from the Shakespeare volumes. The immediate and crucial recognition for Olson —now generally assumed by students of Melville—was that Melville had utilized his reading (especially of Shakespeare and the Bible) to create *Moby-Dick*. As he writes in *Call Me Ishmael*: "Melville's reading is a guage of him, at all points of his life. He was a skald, and knew how to appropriate the work of others. He read to write."[44] As we shall see, the statement also holds true for both Dahlberg and Olson.

Olson was not able to pursue his research without putting a grave financial strain on his parents. While he was searching out Melville's library in 1934, he became an Instructor of English at Clark University in Worcester, where he taught Freshman English, coached the debating teams, and assisted with the dramatics club.

In August of 1935 his father died. The loss was crushing to the son who could not help feeling guilty that he perhaps had been partly responsible for his death. They had not parted on good terms:

> ...it was from Gloucester that he left the last time I saw him whole. He was to go the next weekend to the Nat'l Convention of the Carriers at Cleveland. It was to be a big business, for he and his cronies around the country (he had built up a terrific correspondence) were hoping they could turn out the old officers and put in Fred Douglas of Brooklyn. It was one of the payoffs my father intended, for the officers of the NALC had failed him in his fight. He was out to get them. It was to be a big thing, and when he was leaving he waked me to ask if I would let him take my suitcase which was bigger and newer than his. I had a use for it that coming weekend which seemed important to me, and I refused. He went away sore, and the curious thing is, that though my mother and I drove the hundred miles to the hospital the moment we heard he was sick

and though I was with him much of the time until he died, I do not remember that he ever addressed me or seemed to notice that I was there. He pinched my mother's nose and said something unintelligible from the twist of his mouth, but it is only now that I realize at no time did he admit a notice of me. Or do I exaggerate and punish myself anew for the guilt of my refusal of the suitcase. I do not know.[45]

Shattered, Olson went back to Clark and finished his teaching year. But by the spring and early summer of 1936, he was oppressed by the need to make some difficult decisions.

He found the teaching at Clark restricting because it left him little time for the Melville research; this probably explains why he applied for admission to the doctoral program at Harvard. He urgently wanted to begin writing; the new material from the Melville library and the family papers was waiting to be used. F. O. Matthiessen, who had been one of his advisors on the master's thesis at Wesleyan, was now teaching at Harvard. He encouraged Olson to combine his writing on Melville with further graduate study. Matthiessen was also instrumental in getting Olson appointed as an Assistant in English and American Literature. Olson was not academically ambitious; he entered graduate school mainly because Melville continued to haunt his memory and imagination.

Since his father's death the previous year, the family's financial affairs were unusually tight. Olson had worked for a number of summers as a substitute letter-carrier in Gloucester. He began the summer of 1936 with the same job. Early in July, however, he managed to take a leave of absence and sign on as a deck-hand on the sword-fishing boat, the *Doris M. Hawes*. The decision may have been completely impulsive. With Harvard approaching in the fall and Melville on his mind, Olson's reason for going to sea may simply have been like that of Ishmael in *Moby-Dick*. Perhaps the pressure he was under on the land might find some release on the water. The cruise lasted about three weeks (from July 7th to July 28th), but it did not resolve any of Olson's inner conflicts. In fact, he received a rather cool reception from the veteran sailors and returned to Gloucester far from relieved of his worries.

He found the sailors suspicious of him for reading and writing as much as he did during his spare hours. While Olson believed he would eventually win their confidence and prove himself, the more he occupied himself with his journal and reading the less he was "liked by these men who respect the hand more than the mind, so that a boy of 14 who whittles out the model of a vessel is more to be liked than a boy of 24 who listens and is sometimes seen writing in a notebook suspiciously, quietly."[46]

26

His journal describes his restlessness:

> Bleary, for me, I continue to be tired in the head, listless and dumb as my problems ashore begin to come back into my muddled head. Intelligence I have, some sensitiveness, character of a sort, personality beyond all else I fear, agility of mind and body, understanding a feminine consideration of other people, but a vitiated will. And without will, head and heart we are only large, loveable babies, not stormy wise men.

But there were other moments when Olson could transcend his own concerns and appreciate the reality posed by the fishermen and the life he was briefly sharing with them. "There's a muscularity about them, not of the biceps, but of the whole stuff of man, of the gut. One and the same *by* Jasily tough. There is a command and thus a dignity about them over the thing we introverts grapple for and miss and call life." A few days out to sea he wrote: "Melville, I think, saw to it I went swordfishing." But the experience was exhaustingg, as a photograph of him, taken aboard the ship shows: his face is gaunt and unsmiling; awkwardly his large, thin body tries to perch, with one leg crossed, on a small keg near the side of the ship.[47] He is haggard and looks uncomfortably out of place.

By August he was back in Gloucester and had resumed the letter-carrier's job. On the 9th he went to call on Dahlberg. Perhaps with a man who had already established himself as a writer he might find the advice, sympathy, and intellectual engagement that had been missing from his life that summer. Dahlberg was a kind of life-line, thrown out to Olson in the neck of time.

CHAPTER TWO

New Friendship (1936-1938)

There is more political energy in friendship than in ideology.—EDWARD DAHL-
BERG, *Confessions*

The mystery of a human personality is intricate and vast. Goethe said, "All
living things enclose themselves in an atmosphere of their own," and it is
just that inalienable thing which is the beauty and the puzzle, the life. To
convey a man's life! That presumption is the creative act. Does it not always
if it is a living thing—and what else in creating its own life, its own atmosphere? I make no claim—I think no claim can be made—to write Melville's
life. All I can hope to do—or any writer writing upon another man or upon
other people is to share with a reader what life Melville has for me. All the
old questions about what goes to shape a human being are raised anew.
What keys are face, race, place? When was the man most and least himself?
No man's values ultimately are like another man's and who shall judge the
decisions men make except in the light of their own personality? Even to
reconstruct the physical body is a difficult task, photo and portraits and
descriptions no matter how plentiful. (Then M physically: his voice: but
how his eyes moved, what his hands did, the textures, and that which makes
a face so supple. . . .—CHARLES OLSON, "Possible Openings of book."[1]

Dahlberg and Olson began to correspond in the fall of 1936. When Dahlberg left Gloucester to return to New York City, he mailed Olson a postcard,
encouraging him: "Remember, start work on the Melville book. I believe
in you + I think I know. The sooner you start the better. Inaction opens
inferiority. This in haste."[2] Olson must have opened up to him, or Dahlberg
would not have been thus aware of the doubts currently besetting Olson.
Over the next twenty years of their friendship, Dahlberg repeatedly cast
himself in the role of the Horatio to Olson's moody, procrastinating Hamlet.

There was another impulse at work in Dahlberg's concern for Olson—
Dahlberg was seeking allies in his quest for a renovated contemporary literature. As we have seen, Dahlberg was anything but a Party hack, and he
would not bend his literary and moral principles to fit a leftist, ideological
mold. For Dahlberg the matter reduced itself to a question of style. He
espoused a vitality and richness of language that his critics felt undermined
the political message of the earlier novels. In writing about his early fiction,

he claims to have "deliberately expunged some of the joys of this globe, sun, grass, river ... in order not to write a slavish book about a society which concealed its filth and cruelty, and that doomed so many of the boys who became vagabonds, pariahs, or hopeless drudges in great cement cities." Yet Dahlberg always considered himself an artist first and foremost, rather than a journalist or an ideologue. While extremely sensitive to political, social, and economic issues, Dahlberg "first of all wanted to tell a story"[3]—effectively, movingly. He hoped to create, as he later phrased it in *Do These Bones Live*, a "warm-blooded," humanistic tradition in contemporary American letters—values that he found painfully absent in the Marxist circles in which he travelled at the time. Some years after they met and became friends, he wrote Olson, with their friendship and this literary mission in mind: "there can be no literature without a small tender group of men of feeling who are constantly sharpening each other."[4]

After his summer in Gloucester and first contact with Olson, Dahlberg again tried New York where he was employed briefly by the Federal Writer's Project to write the literature section of the Writer's Project Guidebook series volume on New York City. Evidently, rather than completing his assignment, Dahlberg kept himself busy with his own writing and never began his contribution. He left the Project in the spring of 1937 after a heated argument with the director about a failed deadline.[5] Dahlberg seems to have welcomed his dismissal. He refused to discuss his failure to meet the Project's deadline with the director. The incident indicates the degree to which Dahlberg chafed at any imposition of outside authority on his writing habits. At the time Dahlberg's creative energies were focused on the critical writing he wished to do.

Through that summer of 1936 Dahlberg read, made notes, and pondered the essay he had planned on contemporary American fiction. When he met Olson he was already at work on an essay on Randolph Bourne, his current literary champion. Crippled from youth, Bourne's brief and dedicated life kindled Dahlberg's desire to reclaim, in his own work, that outspoken idealism and intransigent iconoclasm that had been Bourne's trade-mark as editor of and contributor to *The Dial* just after World War I. Bourne's unflagging thrusts at the sacred cows of America—from the Academy to super-patriotism—were part of the concerns Dahlberg felt moving in himself.

The essay on Bourne, when it appeared in 1941 in *Do These Bones Live*, challenged, as did Bourne, all "causes and ideologies," all "the canting stones of the STATE": "All dogmas lead men right back to the Abyss; doctrine is the enemy of vision and the denial of the past."[6] By this point (1941),

29

Dahlberg's renunciation of any ties with the Left was total, and his affirmation of "individual identity" was absolute:

> to each man who craved breath, memory, bread, stars, moon and earth, his one and only living truth is: "I AM SOCIETY." Tear the flesh of any of these personal, unique and celebrated I's, place ONE in chains, in prison or on the rack, and you bleed the consciousness of Man. Society rests upon this towering I, and the very holiness of the life impulse lies in the truth that the parts are greater than the whole.[7]

For Dahlberg, who was attempting to redefine his own political beliefs after his break with the Left, the question of establishing for himself a living body of truth was essential. From Bourne, the avenues of idealism led Dahlberg inevitably back to that other renegade of American anarchism: Thoreau. In 1937, slightly under a year after he had begun writing on Bourne, he wrote his friend, Dorothy Norman:

> Have been working on the Thoreau piece.... My whole feeling is that, as it is, we eat life. Man has always devoured man—for a cause, a principle. Causes must fulfill, not sacrifice us. I hate sacrifices, and I fly from the man or woman who has sacrificed himself or herself. Spare me the woman, man who says: "I would give my arm for you!" Spare me the principle which demands: give your life for me.[8]

While he was arriving at conclusions about his stance with regard to political conditions, Dahlberg was also defining the position he wanted to maintain as a critic of his culture and literature. Here, too, the way for Dahlberg could not be ordinary or prescribed. The chances he imagined himself to be taking had to be large, and thoroughly idiosyncratic. *Do These Bones Live* was already beginning to take shape; and, in the writing of it, he hoped to identify himself and his positions. He told Mrs. Norman:

> I am evolving for myself a quixotesque faith in literary criticism. For I am a Cervantist in imaginative belief. An heroical impossibilism is my credo. Am now writing and rewriting my foreward, a criticism, and a denunciation of "relative truths and values" in literary criticism.[9]

Much later in his life Dahlberg looked back on the artistic predicament confronting him in the years 1936-1937. He wrote, "I had not even begun my apprenticeship. It took more than the strength of the phoenix for me to raise my maimed pinions from the ashes of my brute scrawl."[10] Dahlbergian rhetoric aside, there is little doubt that these years were crucial in forcing a realignment of his values. His liberation from any obligations to external demands on his creative energies afforded him the means to scrutinize all that fell within the scope of his vision according to what were, for him, personal truths. Dahlberg chose Bourne to guide him during this period of gestation, "as Virgil led Dante from one fiery circle to another, through the infernal limbo of American Culture where Thoreau, Melville, Whitman still clamour for the ripe warm light of this world."[11] It was nothing short of a complete literary reawakening that Dahlberg was attempting to bring about in himself and his audience. And Olson joined him on his journey.

Perhaps Olson showed Dahlberg his thesis on Melville. Certainly the subject of it came up frequently in their conversations during August of 1936. Dahlberg mentions Melville for the first time in his correspondence to Stieglitz in September of that year. And there is Dahlberg's inscription of a copy of *From Flushing to Calvary* which underscores Dahlberg's new interest:

> For Charles Olson,
> as a memento of our "Melville
> conversations," with friendship—
>
> > Edward Dahlberg
> > N. Y. C. Sept. 1936[12]

Olson's discovery of the bond that existed between Shakespeare and Melville became a seminal insight to Dahlberg throughout *Do These Bones Live*. Melville's link to Shakespeare demonstrated to Dahlberg the American artist's need to be influenced by a great master of the past. In one place Dahlberg would later credit his friend Theodore Dreiser with teaching him "how to read Shakespeare." Dahlberg claimed that he learned from Dreiser to see "all the plays [as] man-eating parables" and to realize "that life rather than the poet had written the tragedies."[13] To Dorothy Norman he allowed: "one cannot know Melville without knowing Shakespeare."[14] But the Melville-Shakespeare connection clearly had been Olson's gift, and Dahlberg freely acknowledged that influence to the present writer: "It was Charles [Olson] who awakened my interest in Herman Melville; that he was brilliant there is nobody save a gudgeon who would question that."[15]

Just a handful of letters from Dahlberg to Olson have survived from the first years of their friendship (1936-1941). None of Olson's to Dahlberg have as yet come to light. The few letters we have from Dahlberg speak with fondness and concern for his younger friend. Dahlberg was keenly aware of and sympathetic to the "seething things within" Olson—to Olson's uncertainties about his writing and his ability to take on a subject as demanding as a biographical study of Melville. Dahlberg referred to Olson's sense of indecision as "inferiority" and believed that it could be resolved only through Olson's complete immersion in his writing. "Maturity, like a maid-in-waiting, will not come to you," Dahlberg wrote. "Besides, all books, no matter when they are written, in what joy or quasi joy of ripeness, are ever anything but mistakes. So don't needlessly harass yourself over the young years traipsing in your bones. The bones are yours and so let's see their signature on the printed page. As I have said; once you get the book on paper, I will see that it gets published. But write!"[16]

Part of what may have delayed Olson's concentration on the Melville book were his duties and studies at Harvard during the fall and winter of 1936-1937. Olson came to Harvard as an "Assistant in English and American literature at Harvard and Radcliffe." He described his duties as "lecturing, reading papers, and assigning material for writing and studying to classes in American and English lit."[17] Along with these demands on his time, Olson also took courses in the Graduate School—a seminar in Chaucer and a tutorial on Melville with Matthiessen.

Harvard was intensely competitive. Olson's association with Matthiessen drew him into the circle of Melville admirers who, as Paul Metcalf (Melville's great grandson) later described the scene, made a salon of Eleanor Melville Metcalf's home on Grey Gardens East in Cambridge. It seems that Olson edged out the others because of his earlier acquaintance with Mrs. Metcalf. But Melville himself commanded most of Olson's energies at this point in his life. In fact, Paul Metcalf recalled, "so consumed was he at this time with Melville, so identified with him, that he determined to become one of us" and was taken in by Mrs. Metcalf to be nursed through an illness, after which he stayed on at their house and simply "joined the bloodline."[18]

Much has been made in recent memoirs of Olson's physical size (he was six feet eight inches tall), his personal charm, insatiable appetite for conversation, and volatile imagination. These qualities endeared him to the Metcalfs as they had to Dahlberg and to most of those whom he met. John Finch, his roommate at Wesleyan, was struck by his dynamic personality, most particularly by his literary obsessions. He recalled night-long monologues at Wesleyan: "The subject, Melville. Always Melville . . . in Paul Bunyan's bathrobe, his great eyes gleaming, his hair crazy like a fright wig, pacing the room in a rapt adagio, Melville in his hand, Melville on his lips. . . . Almost any words out of the Pequod's long voyage." Olson would quote, and "then the hand, book and eyes and hair would soar and wave, the blue bathrobe would cut a caper, and Charlie would holler, 'That's prose, Finch! Prose is the stuff! Match that in poetry. See, you can't do it! Yah, yah, you can't do it!'"[19]

The atmosphere at Harvard and in Cambridge finally became intolerable for Olson. He knew his ambitions lay, not with the academy and its demands, but rather with his own awakening aspirations as a writer. Dahlberg encouraged him on this score, warning Olson, to guard against the dissipation of his creative energies by the demands of his academic obligations. During Olson's Harvard years (1936-1939) Dahlberg served as a reminder to Olson of the real possibility of artistic independence. Olson recognized the practical advantages of working towards his doctorate; though his mother received a pension after Karl's death, Olson did bear the weight of responsibility for her. But when other means of support presented themselves, and he found that he could devote his full attention to his writing, Olson quickly left the University and the Boston area.

Near the end of 1936, Olson visited Dahlberg in New York. There Dahlberg introduced him to Alfred Stieglitz at the photographer's gallery, An American Place. Dahlberg had been Stieglitz's frequent guest at the gallery in recent years, and Dahlberg revered the aging artist, whom he regarded as the surviving spirit of the age of Bourne. For Dahlberg, Stieglitz continued to be a vital reminder of the same dauntless faith Bourne placed in the value of art as a civilizing instrument. Stieglitz championed American artists such as John Marin, Mardsen Hartley, and Georgia O'Keeffe long before their works became fashionable. Throughout his later life, Stieglitz supported and struggled to call attention to neglected American artists. An American Place was not, finally, a gallery but a gathering place for artists and a continuing symposium on the arts.[20] On visits to An American Place Dahlberg encountered many of the most important writers of the period—Sherwood Anderson, Theodore Dreiser, William Carlos Williams, and others. It was to such figures as these that Dahlberg now introduced Olson.

Around this same time Dahlberg also introduced Olson to Waldo Frank. Frank had worked with Dahlberg on the organization of the Writers Congress and was one of the few radical writers with whom Dahlberg had remained on good terms. The acquaintance with Frank became helpful for Olson two years later when Frank sponsored Olson's application for a Guggenheim. Dahlberg actively advocated Olson to Frank, writing him that Olson "has remarkable texture and form as a human being . . . through men like Olson your work will be given the memory and appreciation it deserves."[21] And in a letter about a week later, Dahlberg again renewed his sense of Olson's potential: "If Olson comes through he will be one of the few rare critics in America. If he comes through!" Dahlberg told Frank in the same letter that he had recently written to Olson, giving him the advice that alone would force this promise to fulfillment: "write, write, write!"[22]

During the late winter or early spring of 1937, Dahlberg met and became friendly with Dorothy Norman at An American Place. Mrs. Norman had been Stieglitz's friend for a number of years and had edited the volume in tribute to him, *America and Alfred Stieglitz.* Throughout the twenties and early thirties she had been deeply involved in the question of civil liberties and the fate of those few voices that raised themselves against the infringement of the individual's rights in an increasingly more dictatorial world. She had worked for the American Civil Liberties Union, aided the Quakers, and spoke frequently for the Indian Independence Movement. Her position, following Ghandi and Nehru (she later wrote a biography of the latter), was one of non-violent resistance to the forces of tyranny. But with the rise of Hitler and Mussolini and the advent of the Spanish Civil War the non-violent position became problematic for Mrs. Norman. She sought to reconcile her feeling for the arts and their moral and ethical values with the realities of human misery; the needs for social, economic, and political change; and the absolute necessity of insuring the primacy of the individual in mass society. The conflict between non-violence and the need to fight injustice appeared to be an especially insoluble dilemma for her.[23] She decided to start a journal, in part, to serve as a forum of debate centering on these problems. She did not hope for answers, she has told me, but wished to raise the questions.[24]

She was encouraged by Stieglitz in her project. The magazine, to be titled *Twice-A-Year*, devoted itself, in the words of William Wasserstrom, to "those men of non-compromising, single purpose, who despite popular pressure and misunderstanding, whatever their sphere or custom of work, carry on the fight for the liberation of man."[25] Stieglitz suggested that she might ask Dahlberg to be a co-editor, and since both apparently were in harmony about the scope and tone of the project, she agreed.

Over its ten years of publication (1938-1948), the issues of *Twice-A-Year* contained works by such widely varied authors as Bourne and Kafka, Henry Miller and Thomas Mann, Richard Wright and Rilke—many of the works of the foreign contributors (now household literary names) appearing in translation for the first time in its pages. Integral also to the first issue of *Twice-A-Year* was Olson's first published essay, "Lear and *Moby-Dick*."

By the summer of 1937 Olson had written a long paper on the Melville-Shakespeare relationship for F. O. Matthiessen. Absorbed by his own writing and by the plans for the magazine through the spring of 1937, Dahlberg broke away for a month's vacation in Mexico. When he returned to this country in August, he went up to visit Olson who was summering in Gloucester. There Dahlberg read through the manuscript with him. The long paper for Matthiessen has not survived among Olson's papers, and thus it is difficult to establish the number and kinds of editorial comments

Dahlberg made about the essay. However, Olson did recall that the *Twice-A-Year* essay had to be "pulled out" of the earlier version for Matthiessen.

In October of 1937, Dahlberg wrote Olson to say that he had discussed the essay with Mrs. Norman. They had decided to consider publishing it, provided that Olson began revisions for it at once. For his own part, Dahlberg reflected in the letter on one direction he hoped the magazine would take:

> Issues are being now planned.... American writers from Melville to Bourne will be given "alms for oblivion." It is our special kind of humor that when an American writer has been dead, Americans are generally literal-minded enough never to question the fact: so that Bourne lies in limbo, his books scattered like the buried fragments of Osiris.... I would like to give something of a rebirth to certain neglected writers.... We are ambitious, but have no desire to make claims.[27]

A few months earlier Dahlberg wrote Mrs. Norman to state his hope that the magazine would become an organ for two American artists, even for one, "without something, we are headed for a dark Philistia."[28] Mrs. Norman did not find the situation quite so precarious as Dahlberg had dramatically described it. However, she too had long believed that ignored works by Bourne and others should be reprinted and thus given new life by being reread in juxtaposition with contemporary works that might be of the same tone and subject. The pages of *Twice-A-Year* provided exactly such a format for reevaluation. Here she and Dahlberg were in accord, and Dahlberg became increasingly excited and satisfied by his work. Olson mentioned Dahlberg's enthusiasm for the magazine in a letter to Mrs. Norman early in 1938: "It gives him a context with both tradition and the present which he as all of us needs but he more because of his intransigence."[29]

In the fall of 1937, Olson became an "Instructor and Tutor in Modern Languages" at Harvard. His function was "to govern the writing and studying of a selected group of undergrads who were majoring in English and American literature."[30] This same year Olson also took Frederick Merk's "History 62: The Westward Movement," a full year course.[31] Merk's course turned out to be the most important one that Olson took at Harvard. Merk's concentration on the overland migrations West during the 1800's were essential to some of the concepts that Olson later developed in *Call Me Ishmael*, particularly the importance of geographical space both in the explorations of the West and the whaling industry's (and Melville's) experience of the Pacific Ocean.

Mrs. Norman was extremely enthusiastic about the Melville-Shakespeare essay. Dahlberg helped arrange for a meeting between them in Cambridge

35

in mid-November of 1937. Spurred by their conversation, Olson managed to complete some primary revisions of the essay and sent the manuscript to Dahlberg in New York. Dahlberg replied that it was "the best piece of imaginative criticism on Moby-Dick that [he had] read anywhere," and that he thought it "a real contribution to criticism."[32] But he returned the manuscript to Olson, bracketing the material he thought should remain and advising Olson, in the same letter, to subordinate the Shakespeare material to the discussion of *Moby-Dick*, a suggestion Olson later emloyed in the finished essay.

In a little over a week, not having had an answer from Olson, Dahlberg seasoned his initial praise with a prod, hoping to force Olson into the revisions more quickly. He observed that "a manuscript in the hands of its author has only a metaphysical existence."[33] But Olson was not able to "recast" the essay at once, despite Dahlberg's pressure.

Olson reported having suffered from "a strange sickness" for nearly a month, during which time he was completely incapacitated and therefore unable to write.[34] Such illnesses often occurred at crucial moments in Olson's life prior to this moment. Olson habitually worked for days on end, pushing himself to the point of complete physical exhaustion and collapse, after which he would have to be slowly nursed back on his feet. For example, the night before he competed in the finals of the National Oratorical Championships in Washington, during his senior year in high school, he developed laryngitis and was barely able to win the third prize. The spring that his M.A. Thesis at Wesleyan was due, he was secluded in the school's infirmary for over a month, necessitating his doing the entire job of writing in one mad rush at the end of the term. His advisor, Wilbert Snow, vividly recalled those frantic final weeks:

> At Wesleyan then there was a May 1st deadline for Master's theses. On about April 10th Charlie called me up at 2:00 a.m. in the night and asked me to come in, if I would, to read chapter eighteen so he could finish it. I went in, and spent two hours with him. Two weeks later, nearer and nearer to the deadline, he called me up at 3:00 o'clock in the morning, and asked if I would dress and come in to read a chapter on *Moby-Dick*. Now professors wouldn't do that for many people. But I'm sure if you knew him, you would do it for Charlie.[35]

Such unconventional cycles of obsessive work preceded or followed by total inactivity continued throughout Olson's life. His work invariably took its toll on his health. At the time Dahlberg was demanding the revisions of the *Twice-A-Year* essay, Olson had reached one of his physical and mental limits.

36

In a long letter to Olson, after commiserating with him about his troubled health and strained confidence, Dahlberg tried to cheer him up: "However, I am not too worried about you. You have an extraordinarily warm and fluid personality to which people are strongly attracted, so that every time the cold blizzards and profound psychic wastes and moraines of Harvard will melt to you. That of course, on the human side, + important, but not the real problem." As Dahlberg understood it, in the same letter, the "real problem" lay in Olson's often disabling inertia, and he prescribed a strong dose of will and writing as a cure: "otherwise you will go along at a zero level + say to yourself in your most dire moments: My God, nothing is happening to me. And of course, nothing can happen unless we make it."[36]

Quite simply, what Dahlberg, the experienced writer, was trying to teach Olson, the neophyte, was the writer's need for a daily routine and discipline. Dahlberg steadfastly observed his own writing rituals, never allowing himself to wander very far from the work at hand. He wrote Mrs. Norman around this time about the Bourne essay, expressing his own state of mind when he was practicing his craft: "I fear to let one day pass without working on it. For each morning I have to begin anew and put my will and eyes together all over again."[37] In *The Confessions* and in numerous other places, Dahlberg amplifies his convictions about the need for daily discipline and productivity. They become more than a simple demand:

Delay is an impostume in the soul. He who does not whet his will every hour perishes of velleity. I have no clear or good purpose save in exercising my will, for nothing I do appears right to me, but I must do it. Unless I go to my table and work each day the stars disappear, the heavens go out, and the world vanishes. He who does nothing kills the sprouting bubbling plants; his foot is dead and his neck is froward. As is said in the Gita:

If I did not always work unwearying,
Men would follow my ways,
The world would perish if I did not work
I should bring back chaos, and all beings would suffer.[38]

Olson was just the opposite when it came to self-discipline and work. Of course his capacities for taking on and accomplishing prodigious amounts of work are legendary. But unless Olson was working, totally, non-stop—whether talking, writing, reading—he was subject to inactive slumps, "strange sicknesses," profound depressions. Olson seems to have functioned best at those intense moments of pressure while Dahlberg struggled to control and order, to restrain the centripetal elements of his own nature through daily acts of will. This was the primary polarity in their chemistries as men and artists. They would never agree about Olson's compulsive schedules. Dahlberg believed he often had to "cudgel [Olson] in order to persuade him to write."[39] This may have been true, from Dahlberg's point of view, but Olson later pointed out to him that these "differences arise from, CON NATURAM, different identities."

However, there was another facet of Olson's character that enabled Dahlberg to forgive him his erratic writing patterns. Dahlberg was magnetically drawn to and had absolute confidence in Olson's "exquisite refinement" and intellectual brilliance. "I can tell you," he wrote to me, "that in his primy youth he was remarkable, and I was certain he was to be a demi-god of our literature."[41] In their later correspondence Dahlberg told Olson that he recognized the spark of genius in him after just a few minutes of conversation at their first meeting. Thus, impatient as Dahlberg may have been with Olson's habits, and as much as he hoped to conquer his procrastination, Dahlberg rebuked Olson ironically, chided him tenderly:

Dear Charles Olson:

I wrote you a letter a week ago, but have not heard from you. Needless to say I am very suspicious of your nefarious silence. Ease my wrath by sending in your manuscript which has become a veritable blockade against all publication, publishing, writing, conceiving, creating, and misconceiving!

Your friend,
Edward Dahlberg

P.S.
One of your breathless, panting pulsating special-delivery letters, would be very timely—provided the m.s. accompanies it.[42]

When at length the revised Melville-Shakespeare essay arrived, several weeks after Dahlberg's note, Dahlberg could find only one word for it: "beautiful."[43] Dahlberg and Mrs. Norman recommended further revisions, but they were especially pleased with Olson's manuscript and agreed to publish it in the first (Fall 1938) issue of *Twice-A-Year*.

In March of 1938, a month after he sent the manuscript to Dahlberg, Olson himself went to New York. There he stayed with Dahlberg and read the latest version of Dahlberg's essay on Thoreau, eventually to become the second essay in *Do These Bones Live*. Olson was astonished by Dahlberg's piece, and when he returned to Cambridge he wrote Mrs. Norman, bursting with praise for Dahlberg's "triadic essay on the Poet and State":

I read it as a whole and it seems to me his finest work. The three parts have each their own fluency. I think the "Thoreau" part the only true reading of the man which has been written. Of course this is so right, that Dahlberg should touch the true tincture of Thoreau. The embrace is primary, out of time and space, for their temperaments are significantly consonant. Dahlberg has delivered Thoreau from the American scholars and their cheeping discord and established him in his context and concord with humanity. The ending of the Thoreau piece and the ending of both "hate and war," "superstition and image" sing the subtitle Dahlberg has planned to give the whole book, "A Vision of An American Culture." I like to think of the "hate and war" section as a preamble; its compactness is artistically as subtle a form as Dahlberg has achieved. The form-idea-and language, elliptical and stranded, is to me completely realized. Ultimately, I feel it will prove to be actually the finest of all the three beautiful parts of this essay that seems to me one of the best I have ever read. In this essay of three parts—the man symbol, the parable and the fact—Dahlberg's prose has a challenge of acclivity which is quite wonderful. His prose has now his own personal orbit.[44]

Olson's admiration for Dahlberg's prose, especially for its personal tone and contact with his subject, eventually found its way into Olson's style in his work on Melville, both in the essay and later in *Call Me Ishmael*.

Dahlberg visited Olson in Cambridge in April, and together they made the rounds of the bookstores and took long walks by Boston Harbor. Later they travelled to Gloucester where they stayed with Olson's mother, Olson revising "Lear and Moby-Dick in one room, while [Dahlberg] was composing *Do These Bones Live* in another."[45] In Gloucester they discussed another essay on "Melville and Democracy" which Olson planned for *Twice-A-Year*. Mrs. Norman was later to be excited by the prospect of this new essay, particularly since it spoke directly to the concerns of the magazine. However, by the end of the spring semester in June, Olson put aside the revisions of "Lear and *Moby-Dick*" and his preliminary sketch of the new essay and took an extended vacation. He hitch-hiked to the West Coast. Dahlberg explained Olson's restless impulse to Mrs. Norman: "He needed to get away from the little aridities of Harvard, to get away so that at least he may have the sadness and the repinings of having been somewhere."[46]

On his return from the West Coast in July, Olson wrote Mrs. Norman to apologize for not having let her know he was leaving and to reassure her about the progress on the revisions of the essay. The tone of his note was strained, and he seemed bothered by a vague and disquieting feeling about "the persistence of failure" in his life.[47] In August, after he had settled in Gloucester, he wrote her again to say that he had been completely disillusioned with the summer's trip, having found little more than "real estate projects or decay" along the highways he had travelled.[48]

Dahlberg was also staying in Gloucester during August. He asked Olson to read the Bourne essay, which he finally had completed after two years of intermittent work on it.[49] Olson was again filled with admiration for Dahlberg's writing when he wrote to Mrs. Norman about the latest piece, referring to it as "Edward's own parable."[50] On the same day, Dahlberg also wrote Mrs. Norman to inform her that "Olson is back and he suggests as the title of the [Bourne] essay, AFTER RANDOLPH BOURNE. I think that it is very good and accurate. My own title for it is now, AFTER RANDOLPH BOURNE: IN THE SADDLE OF ROZINANTE."[51] Thus, a critical exchange had developed between the two men, with Olson offering his advice to Dahlberg and to a degree helping Dahlberg with some of his own creative decisions.

When Dahlberg left Gloucester at the end of August, however, Olson had not yet begun the final revisions for the "Lear and Moby-Dick" essay. Through most of September, Olson was flooded by a series of "frantic" personal problems that kept him away from the essay until just a few days before the October 1st deadline. Olson drew a dramatic picture of his latest moment of crisis. The difficulties were over money matters, both at home and at Harvard where Olson had not left his affairs in order before leaving on his vacation. He was completely unnerved by the experience: "To come back here, find my mother upset, find my friends without jobs or money, and find myself moved out into a hall was all distraught."[52] It was, he told Mrs. Norman, "one of those personal and intimate things which demand all your attention instantly like death."[53]

Another occurrence added to the already chaotic atmosphere. A series of editorial disagreements had led Mrs. Norman and Dahlberg to the point where they both agreed they could no longer work together in harmony on the magazine. Though Stieglitz attempted to reconcile them, the disagreement proved to be too wide to be bridged. Dahlberg did not return to New York, but stayed in a Boston rooming house. He assured Mrs. Norman that he was not "cankering over our differences." Instead, he went on to write in the same letter, "I feel in myself a mournful and misty loneliness that is not too remote from a sad and sweet serenity. With the tumult of JOB and Ezekiel in me I am making ready to write again of America, Do these bones live?"[54]

In *Do These Bones Live* Dahlberg writes of the creative imagination: "Criticism, painting, poetry, is but deeply awakened self-love. AMOR FATI, to love one's fate and truths, and he who does not love his own truths, absolutely, would be more truthful if he kept silent."[55] In Dahlberg's and Mrs. Norman's unwillingness to compromise a single point of principle in their editorial misunderstandings we witness intransigence in operation. In the above letter Dahlberg seems to be embracing that "fate" as an outcast writer which he was to speak so often about in his later works. He now chose the solitude and anonymity of the boarding house rather than suffer what to him would have been a capitulation.

When Mrs. Norman offered to acknowledge publicly Dahlberg's help with the magazine, he replied in tones that illustrate the self-isolating and self-sufficient aspects of his character. The words were calm and revealing:

> As for giving me credit for whatever help I gave, no, please don't; believe me, finally, that kind of thing does not greatly matter to me; I pine as much for darkness as I do for the heady and glaring light; I have both in me, of course, but I struggle against the one by wooing the other, sweet and darksome limbo. So do not let that concern you; it is really all right, as it is, with me.[56]

Dominant in his concerns, however, remained Dahlberg's interest in helping his friend Olson. He went on in the same letter:

> I have a letter, special, from Olson; he is distraught as who is not; he will very likely be in Boston Saturday and I will go over Lear and Moby-Dick and compress it as best I can so that you will have a clean and beautiful essay for the magazine. It is a lovely essay, Dorothy; I have read just about everything that has been written about Herman Melville as I am making ready to do my piece on him—his is the best that has come out of this country. Believe me, I do not exaggerate, never with my friends, never; but I am also not afraid to praise them long before they become the meretricious myths that Americans make them into when they trouble to do so at all.[57]

Olson and Dahlberg did meet, and with the editorial advice from Dahlberg, Olson returned with the essay to Gloucester. Through the rest of September and a series of somewhat comic and melodramatic situations (at one point Olson was typing the manuscript in the back seat of an automobile during a torrential rainstorm) and a flurry of those "breathless, panting" letters and telegrams to Mrs. Norman, Olson just managed to get the manuscript to the printer before the shop closed on September 30th, the night before the deadline.[58] Though anxious through most of September, Mrs. Norman took Olson's cliff-hanging with good humor and in fact paid him an advance for his work to ease his fiscal crisis a bit.

"Lear and Moby-Dick" represents Olson's first attempt to shape the material he discovered in Melville's personal library nearly four years earlier. While in his Wesleyan Master's thesis Olson could only guess at the attraction of Melville for the Elizabethans in general and for Shakespeare in

41

particular, the first paragraph of the published essay declared the connection with authority:

> I propose a Melville whose masterpiece, *Moby-Dick*, was actually pre-cipitated by Shakespeare. Shakespeare's plays became a great metaphor by which Melville objectified his own original vision. What was solvent within Melville Shakespeare, in the manner of a catalytic agent, precipitated. Melville had brought his first five books out of suspension but the constant if subtle presence of Shakespeare in *Moby-Dick* and Pierre suggests that Melville needed just the fine metal of Shakespeare.[59]

The assertions here need only be briefly set against the last paragraph of Olson's introduction to the Master's thesis for the reader to sense the freedom Olson was enjoying in the *Twice-A-Year* essay. The introduction to the thesis closes:

> This study, then ... humbly seeks to take a few corrective steps. This is not the story of his life, but of his work and thought. Biography and praise are minimized. Boldly the position of Melville with Whitman, Thoreau, Hawthorne, Emerson, and Poe is assumed. The thesis consists of analyses of his prose works as they appeared, with his actions and reading dovetailed in between. Experience is added only where it is the all-important key. The presentation is as exact as possible after the ravage of the years on the actual facts. ... If this thesis but redirects Melville scholarship, it will have served.

Admittedly, Olson had had to please other critical opinions than his own in "The Growth of Herman Melville." However, the intervening years, the closeness to Dahlberg in the writing of the essay, the exposure provided by the magazine, and, above all, the discovery of the Shakespeare notes all helped Olson to ripen his vision of Melville and his masterpiece.

Olson's intention in the essay was to reveal, primarily through the Shake-speare annotations, Melville's state of mind and spirit in the composition of *Moby-Dick*. In the first part of the essay Olson documents Melville's own agonized quest for answers to philosophical riddles, those ambiguities of good and evil, the benign and simultaneously savage nature of the universe. Shake-speare "fixed and fascinated Melville" because he dealt with those forces of blackness" and thus held Melville by his "flashings-forth of the intuitive Truth in him; those short, quick probings at the very axis of reality."[60] Melville's preoccupation with "madness, villainy and evil" in *Moby-Dick* could now be traced to the marginalia in the last volume of his Shakespeare set, which included *Othello, Hamlet*, and *King Lear*.

The second and third sections of the essay establish the links between Melville's marginal notes and the structure of *Moby-Dick*. Olson's emphasis here is on the particular use Melville made of *Lear* in the creation of analagous characters (Pip emerges from the Fool; Ahab is cut from the same cloth as one of Shakespeare's arch-villains, an Edmund or a Regan). Throughout Olson maintains that Shakespeare's influence inspired Melville and "lead into the splintered heart of *Moby-Dick*." Ahab's madness draws energy from Lear's, and the ambience of the novel, Olson argues, was "conceived . . . as dark and tragic."

It is in the second and third sections that Olson is at his strongest. In his treatment of Melville's reading of Shakespeare the essay springs to life and we, too, seem to read the play with Melville. The force of Olson's presentation resides in the subtle inter-weavings of Melville's notes to the play and Olson's reflections on how they manifested themselves in Melville's thought. The transferences from the play to the novel are made with fluid ease. The tone is lively, splendidly personal. Olson is not concerned with documentation when he writes:

Albany is a Starbuck,—and not in such men, guarded against life as they are by the protective tissue of accepted morality, did Melville look for answers. He turned rather to men who like Job suffered—to Lear and Edgar and Gloucester. Judged by his markings upon the scene in which Edgar discovers, with a hot burst in his heart, his father's blindness, Melville perceives what suggests itself as a symbol so inherent to the play as to leave one amazed it has not been more often observed by the critics,— that to lose the eye and the capacity for sight, to lose the physical organ, "vile jelly," is to gain spiritual precipience. The crucifixion in Lear is not of the limbs on the crossbeam, but of the eyes put out, the eyes of pride, which confuse the feeling and smother emotions. Lear himself, in the storm speech to the "Poor naked wretches," senses it, but Gloucester blind speaks it: "I stumbled when I saw." Gloucester aches to see his son Edgar again without knowing that poor Tom is his son, he has his wish—"to see thee in my touch." He gives Tom his purse and gives him the words of a lesser Lear who senses now with spiritual sight and knows what wretches feel:

> Let the superfluous and lust-dieted man,
> That slaves your ordinance, that will not see
> Because he does not feel, feel your pow'r quickly.

Melville checks this speech and within it underscores "*that will not see Because he does not feel.*" In little, this is the purgatorial dispensation of the whole play. Melville finds in this dispensation, in the stricken goodness of Gloucester and Edgar, who in suffering feel and thus probe more closely to the truth, the echo of himself in Shakespeare. His ponderous heart feels the agony of life. The necessity of feeling, the fertility of the heart for the head, gives all life and point to Melville's criticism and creation. He understood what Keats meant when he called the Heart the Mind's Bible.[61]

In the preceding passage we can begin to understand what led Dahlberg to call the final version of the essay "beautiful." Olson's stress on the relation of "feeling" to the creative act, of the way to "truth" through "suffering," were among the many insights of the essay with which Dahlberg was in complete accord. Later Dahlberg offered similar perceptions in *Do These Bones Live*.

The fourth section of Olson's essay discussed *Moby-Dick* as a tragedy, in "structure and device, theory and characterization, drawing always on the matter and manner of tragedy...from Shakespeare." The final section added another dimension to Olson's over-all view of the novel. Here, he characterized the novel as a "democratic prose tragedy" and represented it as a kind of political allegory. Given the idealistic concerns of *Twice-a-Year*, one can easily see why this general outlook was most welcome. In Olson's analysis of the larger meanings of the book, Ishmael is not Melville. Rather, he functions as a chorus to express the "common humanity" of "a crew which is the census of the world...an embassy of the human race to the democratic assembly not of the Constituante, but of God."[62] Ahab's "solipsistic" evil consumes the democratic world of the *Pequod* and Olson has Melville framing this tragedy in a cosmos in which an egalitarian God allows such a catastrophe to happen:

> Melville wanted to think that the Declaration of Independence gave him more searoom in which to tell the truth...but he learned that such "freedom," of itself, did not follow America's political independence....
> Democracy, to Melville, merely gave man his chance to be just—in politics, society *and* intimate human relations.... he asks that America recognize "those writers who breathe that unshackled, democratic spirit of Christianity in all things." He weds democracy with Christianity because be seems to see both ideally freeing man from his own and his fellow's oppression, leaving man "unshackled."[63]

The wider political focus Olson took in his concluding section on the Shakespeare-Melville relationship, relevant as they were to the concerns of the magazine, seem to indicate the effects of Olson's and Dahlberg's friendship at the time. Both were concerned in bringing a fresh awareness of the relevance of writers of the past to present conditions. Dahlberg had projected this concern in the Bourne essay, and in "Lear and *Moby-Dick*" Olson was establishing a more comprehensive meaning of the novel:

> For Melville, in *Moby-Dick*, to the making of which Shakespeare was so important, delivers the American spirit he got from his times and the

democratic ideal, unshackled and Christian over to Man. The "lamb" Melville thought spotless may, to him, be that Lamb of God, Christ, and he may, out of the America of 1850, choose to call humanity "democratic." But we must finally free that vision from such vocabulary to possess its whole truth. At the end of the book, in the heart of the Whale's destruction, the crew and Pip and Bulkington and Ahab all lie down together, "all scatt'red in the bottom of the sea." They *are* all citizens, their state is humanity, and what they find, in tragedy, is that the "humanities" are their kingship and their glory. The citizenship of human suffering, which is of no country, neither kingly caste nor representative government, gives *Moby-Dick* its meaning, as it does *Job* or *Lear*. For human storms are the stuff of creation. Shakespeare knew it deeply and from that man Melville learned.[64]

Dahlberg wrote to Stieglitz, just before the essay came out, to say that "Lear and Moby-Dick" was "the loveliest piece of imaginative acclivity done on that magical and most misapprehended book."[65] The essay proved to be a success for Olson, perhaps the decisive factor in his being awarded a Guggenheim fellowship the following spring.

Olson's nervous energy was raised to a fever pitch by the final spurt of work on "Lear and *Moby-Dick.*" His excitement carried over into October and probably motivated his impulsive complaints to Mrs. Norman about the distribution of the magazine. He was in such a hurry, she told me, that he couldn't understand why the magazine could not be out when it had not even returned from the printers.[66] His youthful misunderstanding of technical aspects of publishing even led to request that he be allowed to do numerous revisions after the page proofs had been finished. And, finally, he wanted Mrs. Norman to change, by hand, some of the punctuation in the printed essay. This fastidiousness about his work would not leave Olson throughout his life. Now, while his energies were at their crest, he was compulsively active. (Later in December there was another "siege" of illness and he would have to stay in bed for several weeks.)

Meanwhile, Dahlberg remained in Boston, helping to ease Olson's agitated mood. They took long walks by the wharves, talked, prowled the bookstores. But despite Olson's company, Dahlberg, too had his own moods to contend with. In Boston he was again put in touch with his impoverished beginnings. The face of a street urchin he and Olson encountered one morning by the docks sent a shiver of anguish through him, reminding him of his own, desolate bottom-dog days. The fall of 1938 was a fermenting time for Dahlberg. He was reading Melville, Poe, Dickinson along with Genesis and the Old Testament prophets.[67] A sense of incompletion nagged him. In the country, in the world, he wrote Stieglitz, man was "fractured," without a

"VOICE" to represent his human needs.[68] Thus he decided the title for the book he was emerged in would take the question of Ezekiel as its title. Though "the man-eating tragedy goes on," he told Stieglitz, "there is nothing we can do but photograph, write, live and be what we are, unfold and ripen, despite all."[69] Out of his recessive solitude," as he characterized it to Stieglitz, came the words that speak so tellingly of Dahlberg's perpetual exercises of will: "I will write and so heal myself."[70]

CHAPTER THREE

Counterpoints (1938-1940)

Love among men [is] the thirst for eternity . . . and whosoever loves another wishes to eternalize himself in him.—MIGUEL DE UNAMUNO, *The Tragic Sense of Life*

When *Do These Bones Live* appeared, early in 1941, Olson's and Dahlberg's friendship had reached an impasse, and they had parted company. A number of minor but irresolvable disagreements eventually moved Olson to break off contact. The silence between them lasted nearly seven years, until 1948. "There had been no fevered or scurfed quarrel between us," Dahlberg recalled in *The Confessions*.[1] But for Olson there had been a mounting uneasiness and reluctance to continue the relationship.

According to Dahlberg, the division came about because of their use of the same subject matter, especially that which related to Melville. Once they resumed their friendship years alter, Olson remarked to Dahlberg, "it is strange how you and I have got to the same wafty bridge."[2] At the time (1949), Olson was commenting on their mutual interest in the Elizabethans and the writers of the ancient world, which both had arrived at independently. In the forties and fifties Olson and Dahlberg were drawn to the same subject matter—the classics, mythology, and the history of America before the great European migrations. Once again, in the late 1940's and 1950's, they found they could share their material openly and willingly, exchanging long letters about the sources and lines of thought they were following. Whether or not they happened to be actually in touch with each other over the years, Olson's and Dahlberg's minds seemed to be attracted, often uncannily, toward similar subjects. Their first fertile period together revolved around Melville, and the perceptions that followed their interest in that novelist represented one of their most productive exchanges. But it would also remain an unhealed sore point in their relationship for Olson.

Olson's interest in Melville became, if possible, even more consuming with the publication of "Lear and Moby-Dick." With the essay done Olson felt confident in undertaking the ambitious project he planned for himself years earlier, before he had known Dahlberg: a full-length biographical-psycho-

47

logical portrait of Melville. Dahlberg's encouragement, along with the success of "Lear and Moby-Dick" as a first public test of his ideas gave impetus to Olson's ambitions. The history course with Merk at Harvard had triggered Olson's concern to include the historical dimension in the study he felt ready for. In his Guggenheim application of 1938 Olson proposed "to write a book on Herman Melville and by way of him and his works, chiefly *Moby-Dick*, to tell a story of America."[3]

In November of 1938, Dahlberg mentioned to Stieglitz that Olson was "having difficulties" and went on to say, "I have been forgetting mine to help him through his." The problem lay in finding the funds so that Olson could devote his full attention to Melville without being distracted by other demands on his time. To this end, Dahlberg had urged Olson to apply for a Guggenheim on the strength of "Lear and *Moby-Dick*." He confided to Stieglitz that he would speak for Olson "behind the scenes," calling the essay to the attention of those in a position to support the application.[4] Despite his own sagging fortunes, Dahlberg threw his energies behind his young friend. In helping Olson, Dahlberg once again found an outlet for his sympathetic impulse to aid creative talent. Dahlberg's loyal belief in Olson's abilities worked in tandem with his larger commitment to literature as an ongoing, immediate concern.

Dahlberg stayed on in Boston through most of the fall of 1939 while Olson continued at Harvard as a "Counsellor in American Civilization."[5] They were frequently together. On the whole these were bitter months for both men. Olson wished to make complete break with Harvard, but he was without the necessary means to support such a step. Dahlberg continued with the essays for *Do These Bones Live*, living in relative poverty and obscurity.

Further, the winter of 1938-1939 also brought frustration and illness to both of them. Olson experienced increasing emotional strain, "the like of which [he] had not known before."[6] With uncertainty about the Guggenheim, Olson tried to allow for the prospects of further teaching to support the Melville project. But, as Dahlberg later reported, the thought of an academic future only depressed him the more.[7]

On the other hand, Dahlberg began the search for a teaching job, having decided he would never do many books or ever be able to ensure a steady livelihood through his writing. He went to the Modern Language Association conference in December of 1938, "hoping" to "encounter some academic from Clear Water, or Paris, Ohio, who will make an error and employ [him] as an humble orderly to American Literature."[8] In Boston Dahlberg felt himself a "troglodyte." The fall and early winter led him to reflect about himself: "It was Gloucester in *Lear* who says, I stumbled when I saw. Well

I am no better; I live with my errors and own my truths. I have no wisdom in my conduct, I have only conduct."[9] His writing helped him somewhat to restore the desire for contact with the active, outer world, bleak as it might be. Just before he moved back to New York in order to attend the conference and tilt again at the windmills of the literary world, Dahlberg wrote Stieglitz in tones less shattered than before: "My book when done will be as contradictory as life; thank dear heaven, I do not endeavor to oppose life."[10]

Some respite from their respective struggles came for Olson and Dahlberg in April of 1939. In New York, Dahlberg was honored at a banquet given by the Friends of William Carlos Williams, a group formed by Ford Madox Ford to provide a platform for neglected, contemporary writers. Three dinners were held to lend support to three unique authors (Williams, E. E. Cummings, and Dahlberg) in February, March, and April of 1939. After the meal, each read from his work to an audience of friends, fellow-writers, and receptive publishers. Olson was invited by Dahlberg to the evenings, and there Dahlberg introduced him to Williams, Ford, Dreiser, Sherwood Anderson, and others. Dahlberg read a portion of *Do These Bones Live*. Ford remarked on its genius and took the manuscript with him to England later that spring in order to write an introduction for it and help place it with a publisher abroad. However, any hope for either a publishing contract or Ford's written endorsement of the book vanished in June of the same year when Ford died in England.

Similarly, Olson's outlook brightened in April when he was awarded a Guggenheim for the Melville book. However, the same day that he had word of the grant, Olson went to bed for three months, suffering from a physical and nervous collapse. The illness had been the result of nearly six months of illness that stalked him since the completion of "Lear and Moby-Dick" the previous fall. The problem was chiefly one of exhaustion, he later explained to Dorothy Norman. Apparently he did not have psychiatric treatment; the doctors prescribed a rest cure instead. But though he was bedridden through the remainder of the spring and into the early part of the summer, he did not have the complete rest the doctors advised until he finally settled that July into Oceanwood Cottage, the Olson family's "summer camp" in Gloucester. Commenting on the period of illness later to Mrs. Norman, he seemed to be more upset with himself when he told her, "Oh, it was all so stupid and really so unnecessary."[11]

The energy gained from their long visits in New York prior to April carried over into the summer in Dahlberg's and Olson's individual work. Despite the blow of Ford's death, Dahlberg completed an essay on Christ and Don

Quixote (titled "The Cross and the Windmills" in *Do These Bones Live*) by October of 1939. Olson, too, kept busy during the summer, deaf to his doctors' warnings that he needed total peace. In fact, he finished a draft of an essay on Dostoevsky's novel, *The Possessed*, and submitted it to Dorothy Norman during the fall of 1939. Olson also reported being "delightfully snared in the Melville book." Illness aside, his capacity to work and his emotional stamina increased in direct proportion to the distance he put between himself and Harvard, which he had left with sheer "joy."[12] The Guggenheim funds licensed him to be "possessed" in his own way, without mortgaging his health, for the first time in his life.

The essay he began that summer eventually appeared in the fall, 1940 issue of *Twice-A-Year* as "Dostoevsky and the Possessed." Olson called it a "kind of testament of my own faith."[13] In later discussions of revisions of the essay he added: "a piece becomes to me a letter to the world. I take it very strongly as a declaration, and ask it to bear a weight."[14] This concern about the moral obligation inherent in criticism was on Olson's mind in the fall of 1939, when he commented in one of his notebooks:

> As nothing which is not worth taking any risk for is very important, so nothing which is not worth fighting for is either. When you write, you make a fight to establish certain beliefs, certain sights and truths which you yourself see and believe ... there's power in that.[15]

Dahlberg, too, had been occupied with a statement on the nature of literary criticism from as early as the summer of 1937 while he vacationed in Mexico. Surely he and Olson had discussed the function of the critic in the early years of their friendships. A section of a chapter of *Do These Bones Live*, called "Sanctified Lies," deals exclusively with the critical act, and its emphases are similar to those of Olson in the journal entry cited above. Dahlberg arrives at the same place as Olson in his insistence that the critical act necessitates personal investment and emotional risk:

> Have we not the right to demand what the critic feels, sees, Absolutely, in this tragic, fleeting and relative world, what he knows, upon his veins and bones. ... We are all FOOLS, we pray, as Don Quixote was; let us not be ashamed and furtive about it, and slink behind the errors—of science, philosophy or metaphysics—that we do not own in the deep-most throbbing core of our cells.[16]

Olson's Dostoevsky essay was a direct application of this impassioned, personal principle in his criticism. Olson swept other concerns aside in the opening of the essay when he claimed Dostoevsky's novel to be a "parable of our time." His conviction was anchored in the pre-World War II present and its ominous implications:

> We are also lost as Dostoevsky's people. Like them we feel we are possessed of devils. We sense a presence of evil so sharply we instantly recognize our own human fear in the hearts of the German people when we hear they never refer to Goebbels by name but always speak of him as "der Kleine Teufel." We have gone so much farther than the world contemporary with Dostoevsky we do not need, as he did, the parable from Luke on the Demoniac of Gadara to create his symbol and his title. Our demoniac of Bavaria is alive and active and a palpable fact we are confronted by every midnight broadcast and every morning paper. And we sense though we cannot, perhaps dare not name other devils, men with umbrellas, men with mitres, men with guns. But what we do not know is how to exorcise our devils, how to save ourselves from the destruction Dostoevsky visits upon his possessed.[17]

Olson contended that "Dostoevsky names us" in the novel's main character, Stavrogin. In the essay Olson examines the character in depth, regarding him as Dostoevsky's focal point in the novel. Stavrogin is neutral, unable to choose between the poles of good and evil and to act in accordance with this choice. Olson identifies the need to make moral choices as the process of taking" up the burden of life." Actions are the consequences and the responsibility of moral decisions. Stavrogin, he says, is "suspended" and does not "move either toward faith in God or denial of faith." For Olson either direction would have been a vital choice. "But to have, as Stavrogin did, an awareness of good and not to move towards it or even away from it exceeds every other moral aberration. He remains an abhorrent Laodicean."[18] His fault is that he is mired in "a swamp of self;" he is "a sun without a fire and heat of its own."

Poland had been invaded by Hitler at the time Olson was finishing his first draft of the essay. In the world's apathetic response to this treachery Olson saw mirrored the ramifications of the cynicism portrayed in the novel, and Dostoevsky was prophetic for him on this count:

> Dostoevsky insists over and over again that man, to be whole and alive, must choose to believe in his own immortality and in God's existence. Man must pledge himself, he must love. Otherwise, forsaking his spirit, he is left with only the self, and the self, like the bones and flesh, like states is perishable. In fact the denial of spirit leads, in Dostoevsky's mind to a kind of self-cannibalism—the self swallows up the whole being.[19]

Olson maintained that man must regenerate himself by opposing any larger social organism that sought to curb that power to choose which

51

constitutes man's only "authority." With Dostoevsky Olson "put his faith in, and made his demands on individual man." Olson hoped to encourage, in the essay, a "dedication like Dostoevsky's" to guard "that essential and precious human power—'the freedom of choice in the knowledge of good and evil.'" Otherwise, in losing the battle to states or to revolutionaries, mankind is locked, as are the many victims of *The Possessed*, in "a blood tragedy without redemption."

In contrast to the careful lines of development in "Lear and Moby-Dick," Olson does not "explicate" Dostoevsky's novel except on the broadest thematic level. Rather, Olson's desire lay in illuminating those connections between Dosoevsky's story of political disillusionment and amorality and the crisis of Olson's contemporary moment. The failure of Dostoevsky's characters to stave off their ultimate destruction embodied for Olson the "prostration in man" in his collapsing resistance to the dictators. The recognition of Dostoevsky's "parable" and its relevance to the present Olson hoped would lead to a regeneration of beliefs that would enable the human spirit to transcend the apathetic limits of the self:

> Dostoevsky cannot lose his sense of the individual man in the social mass, for he knows that, in the family and in the State, like sins produce like tragedies. Nor can we: the assasination of Roehm and the bombing of Norway are joined implacably together. To establish and sustain his spirit man must live and judge by it. We have need of a dedication like Dostoevsky's. We may despair, but as Stavrogin sensed, indignation and shame are available when despair is felt. Possessed of them we can free ourselves of our public and private devils, for both struggles have, as Dostoevsky knew, inevitably only one ground—man's individual spirit.[20]

At the time of Olson's work on the Dostoevsky essay, Dahlberg too was studying Dostoevsky, as well as Tolstoy and other Russian writers. The "humanity" of Russian literature became one of Dahlberg's comparative measures for nineteenth-century American writers throughout *Do These Bones Live*. As with Melville, there was overlapping interest between Olson and Dahlberg in the background of "Dostoevsky and The Possessed." Similarly, Dahlberg's earlier hostility to the institution of the state in his essay on Bourne echoes in Olson's views in the Dostoevsky piece. It is impossible to establish and prove a direct line of influence from Dahlberg to Olson in the Dostoevsky essay. What is observable here is a creative relationship, a willing coalition of imaginative identities. That both men tapped the same resource marks the richness of these sources and their attractive power. As Dahlberg insisted in a letter to Olson, it was not important to determine who influenced whom. Of primary importance was that the work was produced.[21]

One passage in "Lear and Moby-Dick" embraces much of what both men believed to be essential to the creation of criticism. It came as part of Olson's recognition of the "usable past," in terms of Shakespeare's relevance to Melville's concerns as a writer. Olson asserted (and Dahlberg later wrote him to say he delighted in the insight) [22]:

> The real burgeonings of the Shakespeare reading can be found in Melville's own conceptions: what is peculiarly clear is that after reading Shakespeare Melville found the shape in which he could make his own vision most apprehensible—*Moby-Dick*. The past—and it included Shakespeare—was usable: "all that has been said but multiplies the avenues to what remains to be said." [23]

Dahlberg also wished to work in the same vein, as we shall see in *Do These Bones Live*, and he urged Olson to use his gifts to open these estuaries of memory and imagination. Dahlberg was particularly dissatisfied with that tendency of some criticism to "embalm the figure in the aural incoherencies of the period and insert him in a historical socket." [24] He believed that criticism should create a "viable present" in which the energies of past writers continued to have life and force.

In 1940, almost a year after the Dostoevsky essay, Olson sent Dahlberg a part of the Melville book he had been laboring on through the winter of 1939-1940. After criticizing the section, Dahlberg went on to affirm his belief in Olson. The quotation celebrates Olson's talents, but in its images and style it reflects the critical awareness developing in both men:

> You have, Charles, already, the Seed, of a Book. You have uttered truths known and knowable only to an artist; and I uncover before your Monuments, Temples, before your Sphinx, as I have so often before. What I am doing is to return to you your own Memory; telling you, what was Foreknowledge to your Self and which in the night of doubt, misery ennui, we forget, and will always forget. Could we remember, continuously, we would be, again, in Eden; with the tasting of the Tree, of the Fruit of Good and Evil, we forgot. How Jehovah looked; how to be naked, unashamed, how never to Hide, as Eve did, after she had listened to the Serpent and Puzzled Adam. [25]

Another of the critical concerns both Olson and Dahlberg shared was the belief that the critic should break with "objectivity" and venture a reading of an artist's personality along with the consideration of his work. This deliberately subjective touch is certainly not an invention of either man, but it was an important dimension in their criticism, and both employed the technique frequently and with telling effects. For instance, in "Dostoevsky and the Possessed" Olson was attempting to bring his readers in contact

53

with the tangible, physical image of the Russian writer when he portrayed him in the following passage:

> Look into Dostoevsky's face in the Peroz portrait, painted while *The Possessed* was in progress. A brand lies upon the temple and the cheek and mouth are scorched. The mark is there, and the blessing. The delicate skin and the eyes bespeak hosanna. A woman in his magazine office saw that face one June night turn up to the tender summer sky as he urged upon her what glory and torment it was to speak to people of a world beyond this. His arms woo'd the sky away, his eyes lifted altars, and his voice, bursting chains, cried out: "To other worlds." Call him Israel.[26]

Olson's lyrical image here displays the vital possibilities—and, surely, the risks—of the critical style both he and Dahlberg were shaping. Critics generally do not take these kinds of imaginative chances. Because of the advice of Dahlberg, though, the artist in Olson was daring to express itself in the context of a criticism of another artist.

Dahlberg also helped Olson to recognize the power of stories and anecdotes as a means of illustrating a point. Shortly after his first month's contact with Dahlberg in 1936, Olson stressed Dahlberg's use of the anecdote and jotted the following entry in his notebook. It is one of the very few records that survive from their first encounters. Dahlberg had given him the following:

> Tancredismo, the 18th century toredor, who stood alone in the bullring, without cape and without sword, dressed all in white, his hands quietly by his sides and confronted the toreo, not indeed to attract his attention, to invite the conflict, but to find his drama and the point of his skill in the failure to disturb, arouse, attract the bull at all! Characteristic of the Spanish quietism: Ponce de Leon, who hoped to stand so breathlessly and unobserved that Death would pass him by unnoticed and he would live forever, a white immortality![27]

Dahlberg began his essay on Bourne with an anecdote. Olson had read it the summer before he drafted the Dostoevsky piece, exclaiming at the time to Dorothy Norman about the "beauty" of the essay and especially its striking opening. Olson had called the work "Edward's own parable":

> Some faces speak out their direful truths. We have had three or more true and terrible countenances, the "ugly" Henry David Thoreau, the shade of Herman Melville cast in impenetrable frost, and the deformed Randolph Bourne, the planes and masses of whose head powerfully fold like the agonies of LAOCOON. Truth is so repellent because it wears the lazar clothes of the world. Thersites can lie down beside Christ and Dostoevsky. The scurvy crucifixes in the face of Dostoevsky come from a

most common and tragic sore—Man. We see this potent parable of the terror of truth—truth twisted by the world it must perforce inhabit—in the encounter between Randolph Bourne and Theodore Dreiser.

In 1918 on a snow-flurried evening in front of the Night Court at Tenth Street a large brooding man met a hapless little dwarf wrapped in a black witch's cape and hat and sidled up against the brick wall to let it pass. Ashamed of his fright he walked and meditated with darksome remorse upon man's pitiless reactions to a hurt and pitiable lameness in another man. Then he forgot about it and dismissed it from his mind until the same little figure came to his door and announced himself as Randolph Bourne.[29]

We see Bourne here, not as some nebulous figure of literary history, but as a touchingly human character. Dahlberg adds another texture to the story through his description of the behavior of Dreiser, whose actions are familiar to all of us in his almost instinctual recoil from human deformity.

In two paragraphs Dahlberg gives us perhaps the essence of his style. The prose is "wrought": rhythmical, alliterative, evocative, rhetorical. There is the note of the archaic in "darksome remorse." It is crowded with allusions and images, yet each sentence carefully is managed and deliberately paced. The epigrammatic ("Truth is so repellent because it wears the lazar clothes of the world") asks the reader to pause and reflect, only to be surprised by the next sentence ("Thersites can lie down beside Christ and Dostoevsky."), and finally to be spun along through the consonantal "t's" of the closing sentence. That they are sinuous and "twisting" is the point of the sentence. And then, abruptly, Dahlberg heads us directly into the second paragraph and the story of Bourne's and Dreiser's meeting.

Dahlberg has called critics "those exalted grammarians of our literature: no galvanism and no human juices."[30] We could not say the same of him. An analysis of his style demands the same attentions we give to poetry. Dahlberg's expectations for criticism are the same as for any other work of literature—that it affect the reader intellectually and emotionally. Again his demand comes to mind—that every author must reveal what he "feels, sees, Absolutely, in this tragic, fleeting and relative world, what he knows, upon his veins and bones."[31] The generic distinctions between criticism and literature are, for Dahlberg, artificial, and hence irrelevant. He replaces them with one measure, one criterion: the writer must obey, in Dahlberg's paraphrase of Keats, "the vibrant god-telling PULSE":

We go to the critic ... to be warmed over in the wondrous priapic fluids of his brains. As critics, their viable sanctified lies," as Nietzsche called art, have the same potencies that the stories of Greek mythology have given to man. We desire the same homeric beat and quickening from

55

the critic that we have from the poet. There are no psychic safety-valves, no separate membrances in and upon which poems and criticism palpitate.[32]

Through his contacts with Dahlberg, Olson was assimilating this central lesson about criticism. In a wonderful letter to Olson, Dahlberg tried to sharpen Olson's feeling for the human bearings by which he felt language must set its course. Dahlberg drew his example from Shakespeare:

> You know how unfraught Shakespeare's lines are; either he Speaks in Angered Adjectives, unfettered by phrasings, prepositions; even articles; or he Cries:
>
> Tomorrow and Tomorrow and Tomorrow
>
> or to return, his spleen is Pure Epithet: Reechy, drenched, murky, without a clinging Substantive. Or when he hazards a Slow Dolour, it is shaped in words of a syllable, in four to five letters:
>
> You do me wrong to take me out of the grave[33]

The context of Dahlberg's remarks here had been in reply to an essay Olson finished during the summer of 1940 as part of the Melville book. Dahlberg went on in the letter to criticize the piece more specifically. While this particular essay has not survived, the following comments from Dahlberg serve to illustrate the nature of the working relationship he and Olson had at the time. Even though taken out of context, his advice about writing is worth noting, revealing as it does the light that guided his own style and the qualities he wished to transmit to Olson.

> Your own sentence here, is balked by flattened verbs, adjectival, with barnacled fastenings of prepositions; redundant articles, and too many nouns. Of course, for the moment, have you lost your own Path; for everything you have done is against your blood. But again, and further: You are, yourself, most magical in the seeming slow line, of short syllables: "springs of myth can mean"; "Dreams stop the machines" (Here stop, for me, is not thrusting enough); "Edenic springs"; "Rappacine in his garden of false flowers"; "we are the last 'first peoples'" (Here you weaken your phrase, so good, with "of the world." You over-burden your perception with obstructive words that add nothing to seeing hearing, breathing. The Verb, as Huysmans said, is the central force of the sentence; and the power of the sentence lies in its Crisis. One begins a line to finish it with a Cry, a Moan; to get to the End. The thing, above all, is to Finish. But see, Charles, how such uglified words impede, subtract:— in effect; like; maturing; in order; accident of the industrial revolution; maturity. Shun, above all, the word, maturity; it is a mare's nest, not to be pursued, mentioned; a gibbet-word. And avoid, definition; it slackens

anger; makes a polemicist, a didactic out of the bursting wrathful tongue. And do not, repeat, elucidate. Speech must always be, unguessed, eliptic. When one knows all beforehand, or latter, or too much, ennui super-venes.[34]

Five years later, in 1945, Olson took up the unfinished Melville book again. In drafting this version, which would finally be published as *Call Me Ishmael*, he reread Dahlberg's letter and took notes from it in one of his journals. Presumably, lessons like these from Dahlberg just before their first rift led him to observe that, around this time (1940), when he was doing his first draft of the Melville study, Dahlberg had "taught [him] how to write."[35]

In discussions with Dorothy Norman about the revisions of the Dostoevsky essay during the summer of 1940, Olson brought up those considerations that were affecting his writing at the time, pulling him away from abstraction and toward a "cleanliness of word and celerity of movement" in his prose. Olson was learning, he told Mrs. Norman, to "image what you feel."[36] The emotional and psysiological impulses intrinsic to the act of writing which Olson was learning to employ through Dahlberg grew to be imperatives, as we shall see, in Olson's later writing. Olson wrote Mrs. Norman a bit later in the summer with a further thought about his style: "I want my throat to be in it, as purely as I can."[37]

1940 was the crucial year in Dahlberg's and Olson's friendship. During the winter and spring Olson was in New York frequently, often staying for weeks at Dahlberg's tiny apartment. He renewed his acquaintance with Waldo Frank. He called on Stieglitz at An American Place. He met the Italian painter Corrado Cagli, with whom he would collaborate on a book of poems and drawings, *Y & X*, in 1947. And Dahlberg introduced Olson to his future wife, Constance Wilcock. Olson was enervated by the pace of New York, so different from the life he led in Gloucester where he often did not speak to anyone for days at a time, and where he found himself, for the most part, "grimly upon the cold table of the self."[38] Unlike Dahlberg, who could work almost anywhere and under the most trying circumstances, Olson relied on the security of one place to sustain his concentration. Gloucester was, and would remain throughout his life, the one place that gave him "location." The weeks he spent with Dahlberg in New York fueled him for the privacy of the beach-side cottage where he stayed, immersed in the Melville book, often working day and night.

By July of 1940 Olson had finished enough of the Melville book to seek Dahlberg's comments. I have quoted from part of Dahlberg's response earlier to show the kind of critical reactions Olson received from his friend. Though the date of Olson's completion of this version of the Melville study is uncertain, Olson recalled to Ann Charters that he had done a "first version" by 1940.[39] Dahlberg probably saw the draft near the end of the year. Olson had moved to New York in November of 1940 to find a job, the money from the Guggenheim having long ago run out. Charters retells the events involving the Melville manscript as Olson reported them to her in conversation:

> The first draft of the Melville book was completed in 1940, and Olson went over the 400 pages ms. with Edward Dahlberg. Dahlberg's opinion was that the literary style was inappropriate—"too Hebraic, Biblical Old Testament."[40]

Dahlberg also recalled the event to Stieglitz:

> I begged him to do something small, not to essay a book in gaudy mural size. Well, I read his MS., which was to be dedicated to me, and it was written in a tumid bathetic Dahlberg prose, with all my worst faults. Aside from that it was vain and ambitious. The titles were Genesis and Exodus and Numbers and so one, and I felt this was just too vain-glorious.... I had to reject almost the whole of the MS.... And so I begged Olson to toil with his book, to cast out the falsely vain titles and the mimetic Dahlberg dross, and find a prose and feeling and heart for himself. But he could not or would not do it, and naturally supposed that my judgement was in error, and it is hard, very, for a writer who dotes on his judgements and work and dances before it even as mirthful David did before the ark....[41]

Dahlberg's assessment of the manuscript seems accurate, as far as can be told from the fragments of the draft that survive. One of the passages from "Genesis," one of these chapters, will serve as an example of where Olson had taken his book on Melville:

> In the Beginning was the White Whale. Melville was Moses, the Pacific his Pentateuch. In the birth of the world did Melville begin, and WHITE-NESS was upon the face of the deep. The FIRST Day and the Morning thereof not the first Night did Melville comprehend, "though the evening and the morning were the first." When God called the dry land Earth, Melville heard not, but like thunder was his ear when "the gathering together of the waters called he Seas." God, not Melville, saw that the Earth was good. Only after God created great whales created he, on the Sixth Day, man: in his sixth book did Melville make Ahab in his own image, after his own likeness, and then only did Darkness be. Night came when man was. Light and white the Day and the Sea, and soil and black, Earth and Night, was man. Darkness was the Seventh Day, and Melville knew no rest.[42]

Dahlberg was kinder than he could have been. He simply marked the paragraph "false bible cadence/mimicry."

Perhaps Dahlberg's cool reception of the manuscript wounded Olson; we do not know how Olson tok the criticism. what is clear is that Dahlberg was pushing Olson to find his own style. Dahlberg's lack of enthusiasm for the work did not fracture their friendship; however, an incident that soon followed, did.

CHAPTER FOUR

"Infernal Cleavage"

I know I care for the man in you (for the author, it goes without saying), but there are many things in you that rub me the wrong way and, in the end, I have found it convenient to remain at a distance.... From afar my heart is full of fraternal sympathy for you, even tenderness.... Once you liked my work, and it might even have had some influence upon you before you found yourself. Now it is pointless for you to study me, all you will see is the difference in the way we work, the mistakes and hesitations. What you must study is mankind in general, and your own heart, and the truly great writers. As for me, I am only the exponent of a period of transition, meaningful only for individuals who are themselves in a state of transition.— TURGENEV to TOLSTOY, November 16-28, 1856

The fall of 1940 and the winter of 1941 once again found Olson in a state of personal crisis. The funds to continue work on the Melville book had been exhausted months earlier. Olson did not want to return to teaching, even if he could secure a position. Dahlberg remembers Olson having told him at this particular time, that he would rather be a fisherman or a ditchdigger —anything—but a pedagogue.[1] He was hounded by debts and doubts about his future. He no longer wished to do without some basic comforts, to continue scrimping, living on grants and meager fees, the good will of friends and his mother's slim pension. Nor could he continue to write while under constant obligation to employers, friends, family. Thus, in the fall of 1940, he moved to New York to find employment and a regular source of income.

In New York, Olson circulated among Dahlberg's friends, visiting with Stieglitz, Waldo Frank, William Carlos Williams, Sherwood Anderson. Olson's own writing had stopped as a result of the move to the city and perhaps because of Dahlberg's advice that he should undertake another, complete revision of the Melville study—a task Olson could not take on at this time, after the energy he had expended on Melville over the last year and after Dahlberg's rather cool response to the work. With the economic and personal pressures building again, there was little left to begin recasting the study.

Olson was staying, rent free, in a room on Christopher Street in Greenwich Village, that Dahlberg had arranged for him with a distant relative. The contacts between Olson and Dahlberg during the fall of 1940 were intense.

Aside from their continuing intellectual exchanges, Olson was also in the uncomfortable position of having to rely on Dahlberg for most of the basic necessities. "I supported him," Dahlberg remarked, "literally clothed and fed him when he came to New York."[2] In retrospect, there is some bitterness in Dahlberg's recollection of his aiding Olson during this time, since Olson, after enjoying Dahlberg's hospitality and help for a number of months, told Dahlberg that he wished to terminate their close relationship.

In later accounts in *The Confessions* and elsewhere, Dahlberg attributes Olson's breaking with him to flaws in Olson's character. According to Dahlberg, Olson felt jealousy over the fact that Dahlberg had written a book during the course of their friendship that made use of materials they had shared, while Olson's own study remained unfinished. Dahlberg charged Olson with ambition and callousness because Olson, according to Dahlberg, deserted his friend for "pragmatical comfort" and "reputation" after the years during which Dahlberg had taken him "under the dominion of [his] identity" and "labored for [his] benefiit."[3] In short, Dahlberg maintains, Olson "had no intention of sharing" the "limbo" that Dahlberg viewed as his own lot,[4] and Olson "simply could not bear to owe the obligation due" to his "stalwart friend."[5]

It is difficult to take sides in the conflict. The dispute went on for years, even after the two men had once more placed their relationship on a friendly footing. Throughout his life, Dahlberg continued to feel the effects of what he considered to be Olson's betrayal; he spoke and wrote about the events as though they had occurred recently. But let me try at this point to reconstruct the events of their "infernal cleavage" (as Olson later referred to it) in order to provide a somewhat balanced understanding of the circumstances.

Late in December of 1940, Dahlberg was correcting the galley proofs for *Do These Bones Live*. He asked Olson to stop by his apartment to read the chapter he had written on Melville, and Olson, according to Dahlberg,

> prowled up and down my room with an animal's jealousy of it, and I was moved by it. I had often said to Olson, and I never gave him nice condescensions, let nature decide who is the better gift; it does not matter; don't worry about it . . . two original spirits are never in competition with one another. . . . Anyway, I thought, I have borrowed thoughts and concepts and hints that are by right and truth his, and so I said to him then and there, I will acknowledge you plainly and straightaway, and so I did.[6]

When *Do These Bones Live* appeared in April of 1941, the Melville chapter bore a dedication to Olson. Though Dahlberg hoped to defuse the situation with the inscription, his use of Melville material Olson considered his own, triggered other and more drastic responses from Olson. Shortly after this meeting, Olson announced his decision to Dahlberg: he was quitting the relationship.

In *The Confessions*, Dahlberg recalled: "he [Olson] came to me, his head pained, the broad surfaces of his face gnarled and warped, and disclosed that he feared my influence was impeding him."[7] Recreating the experience, Dahlberg went on to say that he answered Olson's decision with a quotation from Gide: "He who fears the influences of others makes a tacit avowal of the poverty of his own soul."[8] But Olson would not yield to this and other apothegms, even though Dahlberg "narrated [Olson's] perplexities for three hours."[9] After their closeness for the past four or more years, Olson's apostasy baffled Dahlberg. The injury Olson inflicted on the older man at this time was traumatic and permanent.

Dahlberg ascribed Olson's conduct to a Stavroginism or a cold, emotional neutrality in Olson's personality. Though he and Olson became intimate again in later years, Dahlberg continually upbraided Olson for his abuse of their relationship. And, in the chapter on Olson in *The Confessions*, Dahlberg writes, somewhat melodramatically: "I have taken the oath never to allow a stranger to cross the threshold of my fragile identity and call me friend."[10] Of course, Dahlberg has had quite a few other friends since Olson, but he endows the falling out with Olson from around 1940-1941 with symbolic importance, mythic dimensions: "Charles Olson abolished the memory of himself and me, hurling the latter, his monitor, into the gullet of Cocytus. Right up to his death he pretended I no longer was with the green leaves and the grass that placate our short bitter seasons."[11]

Dahlberg's statements about friendship and influences in *Do These Bones Live* add to the understanding of the importance he attached to his relationship with Olson. The book, it should be remembered, was written while Dahlberg and Olson were closely associated; and, in a sense, the book is one product of their symbiosis. Olson had, in fact, suggested the arrangement of the chapters of the book, as well as offering other textual revisions.[12] It would be interesting to speculate on the kind of book *Do These Bones Live* would have been without the influence of Olson in its composition; unfortunately, if there were drafts of the book with Olson's comments, they have not survived.

In *Do These Bones Live*, Dahlberg frequently argues that the reason nineteenth-century American authors (e.g., Melville, Poe, Whitman, Dickinson, Thoreau) never succeeded in forging a viable literary tradition in their lifetimes was because they "lived in the sanctuary of their own sealed redoubts. Each was an original Monad, uninfluenced by the other. The four or five beauteous spirits of our nineteenth century were only dimly aware of one another's existence."[13] The human contact Dahlberg believed to be necessary between writers, if their work was to develop, was poignantly illustrated by the fact that Melville, due to his lack of both an audience and friends, inscribed one of his last books as "Alms for oblivion." Dahlberg, in later years, grew to regard Melville's friendless predicament as his own, and titled a bok of his own reminiscences, *Alms for Oblivion*. And, in a letter to Olson, after their reuniting following six years of silence, Dahlberg took up the theme again, insisting: "There can be no literature without a small tender group of men of feeling who are constantly sharpening each other."[14] In an earlier letter he had elaborated forcefully on the supreme value he attached to friendship between artists:

> You cannot have a culture in a land, especially in this mechanical, doomsday country, where everybody is so viley separated, and each man spills his spirit like the defiled seed of Onan. Poe could not go to the Quacks of Helicon, nor could Melville, and neither had any real unfolding. Man must talk to man, if there is to be a vision and a human spirit;—otherwise everything is in the hands of the Barabbas, the poetry, the handicrafts, and the thievish loaves. Could not Christ and twelve ignorant fishermen produce a legend![15]

In *Do These Bones Live*, Dahlberg identifies the American artist with the Old Testament figure of Ishmael—an exile, doomed to be separated from his spiritual source, a lonely wanderer. The equation of Melville with the narrator of *Moby-Dick* is an imaginative connection that had probably come up in Dahlberg's and Olson's discussions of the novelist. Symbolically, the isolation of Melville, his character Ishmael, and the old Testament figure, fascinated Dahlberg by its uncanny coincidence—he felt, as Edmund Wilson calls it, the "shock of recognition." Out of these multiple associations, Dahlberg created one of the central perceptions of *Do These Bones Live*:

> American Ishmaels are our artists,—"Call me Ishmael," prophetically utters Herman Melville in the first line of MOBY-DICK—doomed to be cut away, afar from earthly mortal beginnings, the human vineyards, the beauteous Genesis of the protean and warming race-experience.... our rarest spirits, no less than the lowly denizens, are finally of the mass, American. New. They have not unraveled out of the magical psychic skeins of the brains of our early demiurges. Poets here are spawned rather than born; they have come out of the ruck, stubble, hoof and prairie. We are the eternal infant aboriginals. Before Poe, who? Before Whitman, Dreiser or Sherwood Anderson, who?... We are image-breakers, iconoclasts who demolish Revelations, all mystery, doubt, confounding legends —to have what? Rousseau's SOCIAL CONTRACT, Thomas Paine's

THE CRISIS, Robert Ingersoll's arid-pated atheism, instead of the errors of Job, Daniel and Luke? Like that gross jackanapes in the IDIOT, we have put the mouse behind the grate that it may nibble away at the ikon Virgin Mary; and after the Image has been gnawed away by the atheistical mouse, what remains? No poets were ever so basely presumptive as the American. The earth-gods, while serving as humble, common journeymen, word-cobblers, image-weavers, prayed that the soul of a Master descend upon them; so knelt and learned Shakespeare from Marlowe, Job, Plutarch, Ezekiel; so issued Gogol out of Pushkin, and Dostoevsky out of both.[16]

For literature and for culture to grow, artists have to build on traditions, to subject themselves to influences. This is exactly what Dahlberg felt Olson was denying by his decision to leave him. Olson's departure broke the tradition Dahlberg believed himself to be initiating for modern times. The notion that Olson may have required respite from the intensity of their relationship, that he may have felt restrained by Dahlberg's domination, or that he simply may have needed time to assimilate Dahlberg's lessons,—all were possibilities that Dahlberg could never accept.

"Olson had to renounce me," Dahlberg insists in *The Confessions*. But Olson's "renunciation" is seen by Dahlberg as springing from a flaw in Olson's character, rather than more natural motives. Olson may well have been unable to prolong their friendship because of Dahlberg's insistence on absolute fidelity to his ideals and person. Then, too, a student must finally leave his master. As early as 1939, Olson began to meditate on Dahlberg's personality. Short-comings were beginning to surface in the behavior of the man whom Olson had lionized in letters to Dorothy Norman and Waldo Frank.

The following notes suggest the limitations Olson was discovering in his friend. His respect for Dahlberg's intellect is still lavish, but the man himself was troubling:

He stalks words, women, wisdom. His mind, as brilliant as western man has known arms him with all answers and all questions. But when he broods, he never doubts or seeks, he provides himself with the weapons to ward off anyone who attacks the vision. Thus he anticipates all charges. The result, horrible however, accurately rather the cause is an exhausting, harrowing insecurity in him, which he really never examines, only protects. If he could only either believe or despair, but he is capable of neither. For out of both as Uuamuno so beautifully reveals, life springs. This man can only, in withering tenacity, stalk after life and because never reaches it stalk finally his own self. He himself is washed by the America he curses, for he too, in spite of the extraordinary mind and sensitivity and, in a peculiar way, human awareness, is starved with the sin against the Holy Ghost—he goes after, pushes, forces, stalks life and never in ease or humbleness lets it come to him, receives. ... He gathers constantly Keats' lovely words of "proving on the pulse" and yet he quotes it because he cannot finally prove anything on his own pulse.

(All this is rigid + in statement cruel: it must be insisted always with him, his is the most complicated tragedy imaginable: his superb feeling for prose [The need in him for the *Word*, actually more imp.[ortant] to him than the act: so letters, so speech].

Ed discontinuous

—he fastens, in spite of himself on *action*: on the professors of energy—the Machiavels + Nietsche's fix him, though he hates the results—what he loathes is something he has in him.[17]

Olson's critique of Dahlberg extended beyond the artist's personality to question the politics and the style of writing with which Olson had become quite familiar. Here was an isolated perception, tucked in a notebook from the fall of 1939, as Olson was taking stock of his position as a writer and working on the Dostoevsky essay revision:

In Ed's paragraphs sentences of truth lie like bright fish caught in the mesh of the net of untruth. He is not the artist of creative, just because he is the anarchist. Like a net he strains the flowing waters of life and catches live things out of its depths—but they soon die, stiffen in the dry air—only for a glowing moment do some of them flash their life only to be stifled and caught by the stiff net and dry air of his anarchic mind.[18]

Other of Olson's private speculations about Dahlberg have not yet come to light, but notes that do exist indicate a probing of the man and evaluation of the relationship taking place in Olson.

Olson was aware that he was deeply obliged to Dahlberg. And Dahlberg welcomed the circumstances of their friendship, in which he could function as Olson's creative mentor and financial supporter. (In fact, in their later correspondence Dahlberg would speak of their attachment as that of a father to a son.) Olson, however, had noted Dahlberg's insistence on repayment of debts, and this tendency to reckon what was owed troubled Olson, especially since he had, at the time, no way of repaying the debt, except through continued loyalty. And this loyalty had begun to erode. Olson complained, "He [Dahlberg] constantly consults the Exchange—what am I getting for what I am giving. Thus he neither gives nor gets—he uses."[19] Eventually, Olson hoped to settle accounts by moving the relationship onto a less dependent footing, but the compromise wouldn't satisfy Dahlberg.

The dispute over the Melville material, mentioned earlier in this chapter, seems to have precipitated Olson's decision to confront the problem of his obligations to Dahlberg. It is difficult to trace all the threads of material Olson and Dahlberg shared and which later found its way into the fabric of *Do These Bones Live*. Yet the connection between Melville and Shakespeare, explored by Olson in "Lear and Moby-Dick," became a potent and pervasive symbol for Dahlberg in his book. Dahlberg would admit, in his inscription to Olson, that their conversations had greatly enriched his conception of Melville in *Do These Bones Live*.

For example, Dahlberg's focus in his Melville chapter, "Woman," centered on the absence of women and heterosexuality in *Moby-Dick* and Melville's other writing. Dahlberg regarded the avoidance of normal sexuality as symptomatic of American literature's puritanical inhibitions. Generalizing from Melville's sexual frigidity, Dahlberg enlarged his indictment of American literature's impotence to include, among others, Thoreau, Dickinson, and Poe. Against the backdrop of ancient, classical, and Renaissance sexual passion and frankness, American literature was a "withered," "puny," and finally perverse thing.

Olson, too, wrote about Melville's inability to write about women in any convincing or human manner. Rather than reaching back into the past to offer a larger field of reference or to view Melville's coldness as a manifestation of a peculiarly American problem, Olson's interest in Melville's personality and imagination had kept him more specific:

> Nor man nor woman did Melvilel know in love. What chasm of childhood where love and hate for mother sundered his, what timidity of blood which bound desire to sister and forbade the stranger's throb, what gnarl of soil and deny of pew Atlantic America infolded him in, who shall say why this man of flesh and evil and dream remained in hidden rite of the immaculate? Flawed he was. . . . Womanless is his frozen world.[20]

Similarly, the perception of the importance of geographic space in history, as a physical and abstract void against which explorers and colonizers pitted their strength and imagination, was an idea both Olson and Dahlberg used in their respective work from this period of their friendship. Olson had been exposed to the idea through his course with Frederick at Harvard. In 1945 Olson maintained in *Call Me Ishmael* that the "mastery" of "space" was perhaps the central, historical perception that Melville intuitively offered in *Moby-Dick*:

> It is space, and its feeding on man, that is the essence of his vision, bred in him here, in America. . . . The sense of life and death that Melville forfeited is one the experience of space gives. The vision of it is *Moby-Dick*, and its savage myth.[21]

66

But even as early as 1938 or 1939, Olson was investigating this idea of "space." The sweeping formulations he made later had not yet come clear, but the foundations were present:

> *Space the great god* and opposite to . . . the frenzied time in which 24 hours become mean assaulting seconds on each: time breeds action: no contemplation;
> *Violence*
> *Cruelty*

And the notes go on:

> What Frank calls the Great Tradition—and what the Communists see as the Utopia—and what the Americans live as the Promised Land: even those who attack it like Dahlberg:—the whole West they build on is dead, and because they dare not shed the illusion of Progress which the West, because it had space, naturally spawned, they do not know it.

> Before Christ, the thing had begun: Plato (Republic follows Atlantis) and Ptolemy start what is now ended: 2500 years is finished. When the World suddenly burst from the cincture of Homer's River Ocean, the West began, and California reached, it ended. What is going on now and shall go on until America is the late Roman Empire, is but the dying away. But while all this dies away, the new life is already opening: and Fascism is its first horrible beginning, god help us.?[22]

Dahlberg also drew on this idea in his analysis of Melville. But once again it should be noted that Dahlberg takes the material in a specifically literary direction. While Olson's interest lies in interpreting the historical events themselves, Dahlberg, throughout *Do These Bones Live*, aims similar material at broad, literary themes. Unlike Olson, Dahlberg transforms history into metaphysics:

> Know true literature by its dimensional signature. Melville's tragedies palpitate on two distinct planes, the renaissance and the medieval. Melville's tempests, upboiling seas, leviathans, have the speech, wrath, blood, measure of a faustian universe. Hamlet, Macbeth, Prospero, Myshkin, are rapturous idiots, dying out of the dimensional world: mad Hamlet, like epileptic Myshkin, already seanced in a Ghost's substance, would be "bounded in a nutshell" to be a "king of infinite space;" Macbeth, surceased in blood-immersion, dwells in a Cave of Terror, upon which are shadowed the eternal Forms; and Prospero lives in his apocryphal and visionary isle with an Ariel, a sprite that had dominion over all matter. The spatial appetites of man are limitless, renaissance: man's brain is the globe upon which the terrains and melancholy meads of brit cast their evening shadows. The pursuit of space, evil—the ontological White Whale —is dionysiac, but the hero Ahab, is a cloven-footed puritan gargoyle.[24]

In the preceding passage, many of Olson's and Dahlberg's talks must have fed into the composition. The comparison of Melville to Faust had been Olson's in "Lear and Moby-Dick." Shakespeare had been a continuing subject of conversation between the two friends, going back to the night when they met and Olson was ablaze with passion for *Lear*, reciting and acting through whole passages of the play from memory. Dahlberg recalls having been amazed by Olson's memory, but the effect of the performance had been to cause Dahlberg to re-study Shakespeare.[25] One must wonder how many passages like the above were due to Olson's intellectual stimulation.

And, finally, to round out this brief and by no means exhaustive account of their intersecting insights, there were similarities in both men's conclusions about the relationship between Ahab and Melville. Olson wrote in "In Adullam's Lair":

> Ahab was the reach of M's life, but in Ahab he died.... There he stopped, sad fool of shaken self. He knew a dearth and feared a death. He had no faith in life, Herman Melville. He became the victim of his own creation. He was overwhelmed in no Pacific, but in the sea of mystery. He called water "the unfathomable mystery of life" in the first pages of *Moby-Dick*. In fright he refused to unravel the mystery beyond mad Ahab. In Ahab he succumbed. But a creator cannot commit himself to his creation. He must cleave only to the Crucifixion of his own life, not to whatever Golgotha he gives his work of people. There is a certain neutrality in living which is the fruitage of faith in life. Christ knew it. ... Dostoevsky did not end in his Stavrogin, but Melville concluded himself in Ahab. After Moby-Dick, Melville's cry of the mystery and ambiguity of life was a lie. The king of him, his soul, found life a nothing. His fear ultimately was his belief: Life was Death.... "I am a nothing," tolls Pierre, recking not Lear's crotchet-truth in answer to Cordelia's love: "Nothing can come of nothing." Eyeless nothing is forever blind. Lear can be broken on the wheel of fire but his bones like those in Ezekiel's Valley come together in the end.... Lear gave up the kingship of Britain, but he never ceased to be king himself. Melville did. The seed of death in him was the BULB OF NOTHING. "Deep down in the gulf of the soul" Melville saw death, not life. Beneath Ahab all Melville feared and found was emptiness.[26]

The flavor of the vocabulary, the capitalization, the inversions, the analogies, all suggest Dahlberg's stylistic influence. But what was not Dahlberg's was the knowledge of Melville's psychic anguish and ultimate nihilistic vision. This had been Olson's discovery, and on it Dahlberg drew to phrase his own conclusions about Melville and Ahab. Again, the results spring from their association:

68

Whatever Melville blessed, he refused; cursed; he had commemorated the suppers of Xerxes, Ahasuerus, Montezuma, Powhattan; his own viands had been mouldy crusts of ocean. . . .

He worshipped an inscrutable creator, the Lord and his Son, but shaped out of an heathenish animal, a fish, flesh fowl idol Dagon; he adored the pure, albic vesture of gentle Christ, the fleece of White which he heaped upon the hated hump of Leviathan.

In Melville, land, light, are forever foresworn. Ahab, "darkness leaping out of light," prowls murdering seas of sharks, swordfish: the Night— "horrors of the half-known life."

Ahab's Curse is his own, pursued till damnation. All the bodings, monitions, those step-mother intuitions. foretold in the archangelical shrieks of birds, fowls, hovering above the Pequod, go unheard.[27]

Clearly, then, the transference of imaginative fuel between Olson and Dahlberg is present throughout Dahlberg's writing on Melville in *Do These Bones Live*. And the figure of Melville provides Dahlberg with one of the central themes of the book: Melville is one of the few American writers to find grace in Dahlberg's vision, and against Melville's achievement and failure Dahlberg tends to measure the rest of American literature.

Again, it is perhaps not important to determine which writer could claim the material and ideas as his own. As far as Dahlberg was concerned, this interchange of ideas was the meaning of friendship between writers. However, Olson seems to have found Dahlberg's appropriations a violation of their trust and an invasion of his literary territory. Though "there had been no fevered or scurfed quarrel between [them]," Dahlberg reports, the fact remained that Olson no longer felt secure in the relationship. The differences were widening between them, and Olson decided to remove himself both from the obligations and the influences he associated with his friend.

At the time of their break, Dahlberg replied to Olson's objections to his "borrowing" of the Melville material with a gracious parry. He hoped to force the awareness on Olson that he, too, was, or might someday find himself to be, deeply in debt to other writers. Dahlberg was upset by Olson's pretense of outraged innocence. Thus, he dedicated the seventh chapter of *Do These Bones Live* to Olson, hoping his admission of debt would bridge the chasm that had begun to divide them. It read:

Inscribed to my very dear Friend, Charles Olson: My dear Charles: Literature, we know, is the art of ripening ourselves by conversation; and originality is but high-born stealth. How much of our talks have yeasted and bloomed this little Herman Melville loaf; and how I have played the cut-purse Autolycus, making my thefts as invisible as possible, you and my blushes best know. But here is my hand with Mephistopheles' orison:

When your own polestar Truths surge upon the whited page, may "God's spies" put the same vermillion Guilt upon your face![28]

The dedication of the Melville chapter did not keep Olson from his decision to end the friendship, and it may well be that Dahlberg's use of the Melville material simply underscored the more profound differences Olson was beginning to notice between them, acting as an effect rather than a cause of their breach. As has been noted, this was another difficult period in Olson's life, one in which he could not rest easy with himself. In his journals from 1938 to 1941, he writes frequently of the need to test ideals and scruples in the active world as well as in the imaginative world of the writer. Dahlberg's paternal interest protected him from the hard lessons of life he felt he had to learn. While Dahlberg withdrew into his own work and could somehow manage to sustain himself and continue writing, Olson was in the process of choosing a more public sphere of activity in which to apply his energies. "Olson wanted to be a *big* success," Dahlberg lamented.[29] But ambition may be too slippery a term to label Olson's motivation. The apprenticeship had simply come to an end.

One of Dahlberg's frequent assertions exasperated Olson: Dahlberg's fatalistic contention that man was unable to effect change in himself. Olson noted the formulation in one of his journals. "(His [Dahlberg's] argument + justifications—we never change—same agonies; same urges, same aberrations, same pains at 40 as at 20. Only we acquire power to illuminate ourselves: our best hope a return to child spontaiety to him."[30]

Meanwhile, as he worked through Dostoevsky for the second *Twice-A-Year* essay, Olson had reached a more mutable and optimistic conclusion: "The saints were right. Change was as definite a fact as walking in one direction."[31] Olson's concern in his poetry, poetics, and essays in later years focused often on the necessity he felt for comprehending life as a process; and his poetic forms attempted to represent this flux and expansion of perception in the way he, as a poet, perceived and projected his reality through verse. In reaction to Dahlberg's fixed position about the potential for human growth, Olson ultimately maintained: "What does not change/ is the will to change."[32]

While Olson's responses to Dahlberg's assertion came later, it may well be that this sense of Dahlberg's immobility moved Olson to chart for himself an opposite course: to engage life head-on. It became for Olson a question of moral survival: "To articulate one's values is to defend and strengthen them. With speech and act the bruises of the world and other people upon our scruples lessen, and finally disappear. Without speech and act, the pressure against the scruples increases to such an extent no scruples are finally left. One must speak and do or one is left with no shred of self, a passive foil of the world, not of life."[33]

Olson tried to reach a compromise with Dahlberg during their long conversation about Olson's desire to break off the friendship. Apparently Olson wished to remain on speaking and writing terms with Dahlberg, but he did not wish to continue with the intensity of before. According to Dahlberg, Olson "wanted a shallow-pated relationship," a "superficial" or purely "literary" association.[34] Dahlberg declined the arrangement, and they parted.

CHAPTER FIVE

Friendship Again

Friendship is no less a mystery than love or any other aspect of this confusion we call life.—BORGES

A man shall be a friend to his friend, and to this one's friend as well. One without friends is like a lone pine-tree withering on a barren hill.—*The Hávámal*

The publication of *Do These Bones Live* in April of 1941 marked the beginning of another period of literary exile for Dahlberg. The book gained only slight attention; there were just two reviews. Alfred Kazin found "a fragment of greatness" in it.[1] Mary Colum panned it, quoting Chaucer's "no more of this."[2] Otherwise, publicly, the book's arrival was met with silence. Dahlberg's re-emergence as an essayist may have been mistimed, especially since he was writing against the grain of most established American literature, from the Puritans to Dos Passos. The book was premature. It was too contentious, too eccentric.

Dahlberg contemptuously rejected contemporary American literature (social realism, naturalism, proletarian fiction) as well as lambasting the personalities and sensibilities of the central figures of the previous century—Thoreau, Dickinson, Melville, Whitman, Hawthorne. American literature was "an oxymoron." With few exceptions, Dahlberg accused, "almost the whole of American literature has been a deep refusal of man." Beginning with Puritan materialism and "the fight from man and nature," proceeding through the nineteenth century and its cloistered, inhibited writers, and finally settling on the "vandalistic literature" of the present, Dahlberg sensed, not a great literary tradition, but rather "the great STINK."

> The noble problems of man, love, anguish, evil, death, are done up,—ay, Madam Bovary, Manson Lescaut, the Camellias, and Consumption, have had to give way to the realism of sublunary decaying Matter, to the hallowed sputum, to long vomiting spells and to THE SUN ALSO RISES.
> In the puritan Christian cosmogony, spirit was not rooted in flesh just as now matter performs and behaves as though mind were not of it. The demented dervish of MATTER goes on, without a past, a tradition, without a memory.

For Dahlberg, our writers lacked the sensual knowledge and openness of the Europeans; the tragic scope of the Elizabethan English, the reverence for nature of the ancient Greeks, and the abiding moral endurance of the biblical seers—all were absent. The notion of the necessity for originality in American literature, to match the uniqueness of the American experience, Dahlberg argued, had only succeeded in producing cultural amnesia. One of the precursers of *Do These Bones Live*, William Carlos Williams' *In The American Grain* (1925), was a primary influence for Dahlberg in his book. Dahlberg credits and acknowledges his debt to Williams in several places in *Do These Bones Live*, especially for Williams' earlier perception of America as a frigid, touch-fearing culture which, in this century, had substituted mechanical objects for human beings. Dahlberg built on the influence of Williams by exploring Williams' insight on the dehumanization of American culture. Like Williams, Dahlberg argued for a humane order of life and art.

Because Puritan isolation and insulation had drained the American artist of his visionary potential, Dahlberg urged a return to tradition, to the literature of the past—to mystery, to the "heroic orbit"—as the subject matter for our artists. All men must contend with the mysterious fates, Dahlberg maintained, rather than concoct social panaceas and quick, doctrinaire solutions to mankind's eternal questions. Dahlberg's prose crests throughout the book with impassioned pleas for what he considered to be these forgotten values as he continually repeats the problem and the answer:

> Dogma and denial, Calvary or Nature, trampled the throat of our poets and visionaries; doctrine doomed the flower, fruit and savour of their veins.
>
> Life brings its own thwartings, throb, grief, light; nothing can be foreknown; the deepest natures are mysterious unto themselves. Christ's personality is the Ache that asked for a Kiss; Thoreau's is the Eye that shone upon snows, birch, leaves, sumach; without remotely dreaming or guessing the Light that it shed. All that man may know of good, evil, god, the earth, his own nature, is hinted, shadowed upon his organs, on the walls of Plato's Cave, or Dante's Hell. What can be ordained? Ask for a dream, an image, an intuition, will it be given? Or a "dram of heaven," can it be had? The Cup, the Poem, the Light, are drunk in darkness, or else how could they be taken? Beatitude, vision, sensation, stain time, place, the flesh, opaque; Calvaries and Infernos are committed in the drained crepuscular light of the Mount of Olives, or with the Shades.
>
> Our poets, communal soothsayers, abjured the very speech, hunger, blood, without which ideals and absolutes cannot be imagined. These star-garbed specters, who craved to plant an Elysium in the meadowy surf of the northern lights, were much less wise in love, conversation, habit, art, than Goethe who said, "We ought to be and remain obscure to ourselves."[3]

Though the prose is exalted, Dahlberg's position was quite simple: our artists, in their puritan antagonism to the body, lacked soul and any moral claim on us. Our critics were as much to blame as our artists, for they perpetuated the "sanctified lies," Dahlberg argued; they gave us "our most craven fetish ... our nativism, our nostalgia." One of the cardinal lessons Dahlberg passed on to Olson had been to emphasize criticism as a creative act, and *Do These Bones Live* was Dahlberg's actualization of that principle.

As a whole, Dahlberg found the situation in American art, literature, and culture appalling; he portrays it as a desert valley echoing with the rattling bones of unread books, isolated artists, discarded ideals.[4] Hence his title and the exclamation at the end of the title chapter of the book, when Dahlberg unleashed his full, prophetic voice, demanding a resurrection of feeling and spirit, calling out in his wilderness:

> O ye oracles and bacchic fakirs, return to these States of Dry Bones. Come back, Walt Whitman, and breathe upon them: shake them into a great prophetic commotion. Ye choric fools and grotesques, Melville, Thoreau, Whitman ... take these slain, bleached bones of Philistia, and drive them mad, make them weep and say to the Heart, "'Son of man, do these bones live?'"[5]

Dahlberg's testament of his belief was too idiosyncratic to attract any wide public notice.[6] Nonetheless, William Carlos Williams, who was friendly to Dahlberg and his work, remarked to Louis Untermeyer: "Read Dahlberg's new book, Will [sic] these Bones live? It seems incredible that he should have had difficulty finding a publisher. It's a book to swear by."[7] But such allegiance came only later. The book sold poorly, and it remained "underground" until recent years.[8]

Nonetheless, four years' labor on *Do These Bones Live* crystallized one thing for Dahlberg. He had found the "voice" and particular tone he would assume in all of his future books: he had become the "Ishmael" of letters. The book itself was dedicated to his mother, "who, as sorrowing Hagar, [had] taught [him] how to make Ishmael's Covenant with the Heart's Afflictions." In the remainder of this chapter we will see the extent to which Dahlberg took on the mantel of the biblical outcast and gathered it round him as protection and persona.

In his first letter to Olson after their break, for instance, Dahlberg describes himself: "I am, as you know, an Ishmael in solitude; for the most part, the waterpots of Cana are empty for me."[9] The symbolic nature of this assumed figure would stand prominently in Dahlberg's autobiographical novel, *Because I was Flesh* (1961). In his writing, the Old Testament figure tends to define him—eremite, rejected, deprived of legitimacy in his native

74

land. In expressing the self-image as that of the outcast, there is a certain pride that comes to his aid. He can reject popularity and acclaim as anathema to him. Material success is to be avoided, since only poverty tempers genius. "I've been writing posthumously for 25 years," he recently told an interviewer. "I'm a mendicant author. I think wealth is a tremendous obstacle to man's understanding."[10]

Such claims for holy poverty figured prominently in the furious and self-righteous attacks he unleashed on Olson later in their friendship. However, the tone Dahlberg assumed in his writing tends to contradict the actual, physical presence of the man, as Paul Carroll's remembrance of Dahlberg intimates. Carroll offers a man who is "tall, dressed in Harris Tweed and silk foulard ascot, handsome with white hair and trim, regimental mustache." Carroll goes on to embellish this sense of Dahlberg's public presence:

> I remember feeling that we were not in the Cliff Dwellers Club overlooking Michigan Avenue but were instead in the study of Robert Burton at Christ Church, Oxford, the late Elizabethan sunlight trickling through the windows, the large, worn calfskin folios of Tertullian, Plotinus, Dionysius of Halicarnassus, Paracelsus. or the gossip of Diogenes Laertius within easy reach if the speaker had need to check some recondite allusion to score his point. Only the cadence of his sentences and cultivated accent seemed to keep Dahlberg's words from becoming a scream.[11]

Clearly, he is hardly the tattered, penurious figure he would have us imagine him to be. The photographs of Dahlberg from the 40's bear out this physical sense of urbane, formal elegance.

Yet the voice of Ishmael that sounds in his works was apocryphal and in many respects, self-fulfilling. The six years that separated Olson and Dahlberg (from 1941 to 1947) were obscure ones for Dahlberg. He travelled during most of 1941, first to California and then to Chicago, at the urging of his publisher, Harcourt Brace, to promote sales of *Do These Bones Live.* Though he did not return with a public triumph, he did come back to New York with Winifred Sheehan Moore, who became his wife in 1942.

In 1946, Dahlberg was happily married and living in alternately New York and Wellfleet, Massachusetts. His aging, sickly mother had come to New York from Kansas City, and there were pressing family matters that commanded his attentions. In effect, Dahlberg dropped out of sight from the literary scene. The years were spent, as he later summarized them for Olson, "by reading the ancients, or walking, or in my life with Winifred, or from the robust adamic laughter of my year and a half old son, Geoffrey, who is a Jew, Irish and Norwegian."[12]

Despite this isolation, Dahlberg had begun work on another book, possibly on a version of what later became *The Flea of Sodom* (1950). He wrote Stieglitz in October of 1941 to tell him about it:

> I am fumbling with a new book, a different experience, with Jesus and Judas, the latter a kind of anti-hero. Using the autobiographical fictional device I am trying to create a character as sick as Christ, and as cunning as Judas, trying to make an Iscariot waltz on the sermon on the mount. . . . This is supposed to be a novel; but I don't know yet what it is.[13]

By October of 1943, he had nearly completed a draft of the "novel" and planned to do another "slender volume on America."[14] He was repelled by the mood the war had brought out in the country and told Stieglitz that he refused to think of himself as "an American." He cursed the arrogance of men like the Wright Brothers, because their invention had finally made it possible for man to visit the full horror of his innate bestiality on his fellow man. In fact, he told Stieglitz, he thought the Wright Brothers should have been "stoned for their idolatry."[15] Dahlberg was so caustic about "trash culture America" that Stieglitz declared him a nihilist and a misanthrope. Dahlberg explained that he was simply asking to be left alone with his own fate rather than to be pulled along and "beaten to pieces by the land or the times or the people."[16]

He continued with his "little book," writing again to Stieglitz in May of 1944:

> I want to get back to the book. I have been toiling with the little book for three years, and am in no hurry to finish it. I check not my grammar, but my words against Isiah, Plutarch, Virgil, Numbers, and if they are right, then I continue. If there are some Towers of Ilium in some crevice of my flesh, then I will leap to these flames. I think that the whole fetish of originality is a piece of American trash, and at bottom of it is the obliteration of Memory, Mother of the Muses.[17]

These remarks typify Dahlberg's thinking. The years would serve only to entrench more deeply this insistence on his working within a continuing, ancient, literary tradition. He would continue to believe in the inevitability of artistic influence and the need of the writer to measure his work against those of the classical masters. Through the next two decades, Dahlberg stayed true to his sweeping claim that nothing written in this century was worth reading or was relevant as a fruitful source for the contemporary artist.[18] As we shall see, Olson opposed the inflexibility of such dogma, and Dahlberg castigated him for his interest in contemporary poetry. While Olson was growing and expanding his vision, Dahlberg was withdrawing and hardening his.

In May of 1946, Dahlberg finished a "little gnomic manuscript, [his] alms for oblivion," as he named it in a letter to Stieglitz.[19] It was around this time that Dahlberg also met Herbert Read, who subsequently provided introductions to a number of Dahlberg's books. Read admired *Do These Bones Live* and helped arrange for the English publication of the book with Routledge & Sons, Ltd., the title having been changed to the words from Isaiah, *Sing O Barren*. The book was published in July of 1947. Though Dahlberg condensed it by nearly twenty pages, it still contained the dedication to Olson in the Melville chapter. A few months before the English publication of the book, Dahlberg read Olson's *Call Me Ishmael*, and broke the silence that lay between them.

*   *   *

On Easter Sunday, 1947, Dahlberg wrote Olson to congratulate him on the publication of *Call Me Ishmael*. He was ecstatic:

> I rejoice in this small, mythic volume. A little book, no longer than the Song of Solomon, Amos, The Georgics, or Call Me Ishmael, is the mead, the honeycomb and the Jerusalem for my insatiable soul. I love a book with no other mortal deposits in it but the pith and gnome and parable.
>
> Literature is the pious commemoration of extant relic, ritual, and you have deeply understood this. No one before you has really perceived Herman Melville, the fabulist ... your understanding of Melville's need for warming, pagan gods ... which every American poet requires if his genius is to have a hearth, is deeply moving and pulsant. I could call back to you so many lines and passages that you have written, so heavily marked is my copy....
>
> Call me Ishmael is a little piece of Melville prophecy, and you have my promise it will be remembered, and with this my affection and friendship.[20]

Olson did not immediately reply to Dahlberg's praises. When he did, a little over a week later, it was a brief note of appreciation for Dahlberg's flattering remarks. The opening paragraph reads, in part:

> My deepest thanks for the bounty of your letter and your generous gestures. It is most moving to me that the book earns your particular word.[21]

In his letter, Dahlberg had alluded to his young son, and, in his reply, Olson compared himself to the boy, playing on the old chords of their relationship. The letter closed, after two short paragraphs, with a simple "Yours, as ever." Olson could not have anticipated the response both his letter and its tardy arrival would provoke from Dahlberg.

Dahlberg was impatient to have his "gesture" acknowledged at once. Before Olson's reply reached him, he mailed off another letter, this time a stinging, explosive indictment. The wounds obviously had not healed for Dahlberg during their years apart, and Dahlberg's attack reveals how deeply disturbed he was by their break. Time had not settled matters between them, and Dahlberg launched a barrage of recriminations:

> You have written a little book of genius. This I told you in a letter that your churlish silence has been a sore trouble to my heart. Your greatest faults are sloth and untrembling bowels. I rebuked you often for your sluggish spirit until you became dainty and effeminate about your time, until you became a sick busy American. . . . I have never had the coarse effrontery to tell another man that I was busy. However, I succeeded in word-flogging you into writing your book, and all the Grace and Goodness and Courtesy in it you conceived when you were close to my identity. The Noah, the Christ, and the Moses I believe you garnered up from the MS which I implored you to rewrite. I knew at the time that the book was to be dedicated to me. But now, because I took you unto my identity, gave you of my table, and whatever knowledge had come to me from hunger and all the mortal and perfidious aches, you have bequeathed the volume to your poor, dead Father; your acknowledgement to me has the same bitter obituary taste in my mouth, because in the same manner of a perverse Balaam and a dainty and vain Absalom that you were to your Father, alive, you are now offering to me, deceased unto your own character and spirit. What is to become of you?
>
> You have not been a Judas to me; that is a warm-livered error; your sin toward your nature and me is of a cold, stygian decoction. Your silence has been brewed in that foss and marsh where the muddy and mangled shadows abide, and is a portend of a stilly and fetid cessation in your spirit.[22]

On the surface of the outburst seems to be a profound longing on Dahlberg's part for recognition of his importance as Olson's teacher. There is the further resentment about his having been excluded from this particular blossoming of Olson's creative life. Yet Olson had noted Dahlberg's influence in a chapter of *Call Me Ishmael*—a dedication that did not satisfy Dahlberg. He regarded himself as Olson's mentor and had already concluded that Olson "forsook [their] friendship for the world"[23] and thus abandoned Dahlberg to a "limbo which [Olson had] no intention of sharing."[24] In a calmer, clearer moment with Olson a year later, Dahlberg would re-emphasize what he saw as the value of his role in their relationship: "You require me to sharpen the poet in you. The Muse will not honor you without me."[25] At the time of *Call Me Ishmael*'s publication, though, the storm clouds had not yet parted.

In a flurry of angry letters, Dahlberg castigated Olson repeatedly for his ingratitude, his "gluttony for praise or reputation," his inability to create anything other than the book which Dahlberg claimed was "written under the dominion of his identity."

> In our friendship I labored for you and not for myself. Even now, after sending you in my first letter good savory words about your book, how do you reply? You cunningly smote me with an affected and fatuous note. I do not know why it took you three weeks to compose so few platitudes; in that length of time you should have done more. What is baleful is that you have sly enough bowels to know that you were smiting me, and it gave you atlean and lofty feelings. . . . In our friendship, did I labor for your benefit or for mine. What was my earnest for being a co-editor of Twice-A-Year: I received one advantage, I saw to it that Lear and Moby-Dick was published. How did I fatten my bloodstream or my so-called reputation when I ran around getting your essay into the hands of authors who could help you. Was it not my mirth and advantage to give you the fellowship of authors which an unknown would have not had in at least a decade. I did not have it without pang and hunger and denial. You had it without any, because of me.[26]

Before Olson responded to the first letter praising his book, the assault was underway. Olson's note was in the mail when the first scathing letter on Olson's "depraved silence" arrived. Before Olson could reply, another letter came on the heels of the first, every bit as harsh. Olson, livid, addressed both: "I am damned if I can see by what right you send me the two letters I received from you today. If it is under the cloak of friendship, then let me unclothe you, and tell you it is not friendship, and you a man without shame."[27] Olson continued:

> So much of what you say of me is true. Of course. It is the easiest act to stick a finger in another man. We are all open, exposed. The shame is that a man like you thinks he has a right to beat us with our own sticks. We are each Euripedes, and it is only the dogs and Aristophanes, he who longed to be the Thirty First Tyrant, who set upon us.
> It is not love you offer anyone. If it were you could not take it back like money on a table. You buy, that's the verb, its tense forever present. You traffick in affections, deal. I would say to no one but yourself, for I would not expose you, but see yourself, once, gently. . . . Of Sodomy you speak so easily, of neutrality, of dung, of death, and it is all supposed to be a 'guilt' we others, who impinge upon you, are the victims of. I do believe we are, but you, unholy holy, are you not one of us? . . .
> Invert yourself, or speak a straight word, a word unfolded, neither of praise nor of your fraudulent damnation, for they repeat themselves and are not very interesting. You can. I've heard you. I've caught sight of the seed. It is nothing to be frightened of, in fact, you would be the terrible creature you may fancy yourself to be if all the mighty armament were based so based, so rooted where life, which others do participate in, is.

They do participate, and that is the confounding fact you, with all your arms, shall have to meet, even with your own death.

Do not ever again, please, praise me, use those nouns of genius and the like, for I am sure I shall not be able to give you back the price you think are love and friendship. I thought once I could for I did not know how cheap you make them, how they have a market value which you, a Kansas City merchant become a mono-god, presume to give them.[28]

Olson ended the letter with the admonition: "Cover yourself."

Dahlberg retorted with charges against Olson's eating habits and his lack of proper hospitality and "breeding." He dredged up an old injustice from 1938, when Dahlberg stayed briefly with Olson and his mother in Gloucester. According to Dahlberg's version, he (a guest) was given "dingy food" while Olson "sat opposite" him, gorging himself on "large chines of beef."[29] He struck again at Olson's material concerns: "You cannot go the way of the world and be a human artist. Nor can you pity the aching denials of Herman Melville while you denigrate mine. You can't be both spirit and mammon save to the low Yahoos."[30] He closed by lashing Olson for this neglect of a friend and offered the following ironic touch:

I do not know what you will think of this letter; it may bedevil you, or you may see, later, that though you now regard me as the watchdog Cerberus baying at your entrails, you will come to understand that I was the one Guide to your spirit and nature and gifts.

You will pardon this penultimate piece if human malice: May God make Charles Olson a failure. May his Call Me Ishmael go as unsold and as unread as Thoreau and Herman Melville. Should this happen, maybe then some day in some chasm where Dante casts those caittiffs, like Edward Dahlberg who was for himself and not Charles Olson, we can talk about grossness and shame and the dogs that tore Euripides to pieces.[31]

Whatever gloves the two men may have worn in their first falling out had been removed. It was bare knuckles now.

Olson cut back: "You anger me, when, in pieties, you trap and hide your greed. Now you would eat my book as you would diet off my father's death and curse my mother for the food she gave me!" And, alluding to Dahlberg's blinded, filmed-over left eye, Olson drove to the quick: "Why don't you ask of me my name? I'll give it to you, and you'll have it all. I am Nobody, he said."[32] Olson's leter goes on, in defence of the less intense relationship he wished to share with Dahlberg in 1940-1941:

It is thin of you to think I go the way of the world because I stay in the world. Or that comfort is the alternate to a cross. It is mechanical conclusion. Your essene rite of self blinds you, it would seem, makes your fine ear dull. I miss active thought, and intent, when you speak as you now speak. You repeat, and in incantations which do not speak but hypnotize—yourself. Brooks Van Doren Pound, repeat, Brooks Van Doren Pound. But what do you know? You miss now as you so flatly missed seven years ago, the meaning of events, of who and why I see. For behaviour is a long bow. It can only be confused with identity by those who confuse the ritual in life with the ritual in individual behaviour.

If you would play Christ, to succor yourself, do. I said as much, and wished it, with my heart, for you. But when you come down and seek to flagellate others with these outworn rods, these pitiful weapons of a literary religion, it won't work. "Sacrilege," "betrayal," nonsense. You kill a friendship when you make yourself so pious. I do wish you'd left things as they were, continued, despite our disagreement, for I took pride in you, valued the many things you'd given me, had learned, as a young writer might, from your critique. Now you must regurgitate.

Have you no sense of another man's memory? Do you know memory as anything other than a rosary of your own acts which you tell over as you walk with yourself, you and yourself in long monkish robes? It's crazy business, friendship with you, a game, I'm damned if I do and damned if I don't. You offered me many things. I accepted them. Obviously I could not give them back in kind. How I give them back is, is it not, to be my way, not yours? If you gave them, now only to blackmail me with them, then, surely, anyone would wish they had not been given. That is why I say I regret you have chosen to misread my note in answer to your gracious letter on the book and to judge me, judge me, judge me, three times down the wind, with dead leaves.[33]

The conflict see-sawed between them until, gradually, the anger of both began to abate. The letters became less strident. First Dahlberg injected a touch of humor and self-deprecation into the exchange. He corrected Olson's assessment of him as Christ: "I do not envisage myself as Christ, or even some wayward or fallen essence of him. I am a sick nervous Jew, a base and whoring issue of Noah, Seth and Japheth."[34] He continues in the same vein: "I have never had disciples; you were my friend; I taught you how vile our coincidental earth is, how loathsome the American naturalists are, and I made you write." And he finishes the letter with the gentleness Olson asked him for:

Charles, we cannot always be as interesting as we think we are. Doubtless, while you were reviling me for writing you letters that were not as remarkable as I thought they were, you were unmindful of the boring observations you were making.

Be patient and ruminative, like Buddha and the Cow. If you are fortunate, you may, after a decade of ennui and stupidity and vice and reading, be able to gather up enough parables and feeling for another small book of genius like *Call Me Ishmael*.[35]

Olson replied to this, "without the humping of the blood," but he challenged Dahlberg's claim to have been the generative force in the composition of *Call Me Ishmael*:

> I think you are quite wrong, "purblind," to see ISHMAEL as governed by your identity. I should myself have to admit another man, Melville. And you will excuse me if I note that it was written by a third man and, unsatisfactory as the book is to me, I have the impression that it does declare a—to use part of a man's phrase whom you introduced me to— "sense of life" different from Edward Dahlberg's or Herman Melville's. The anthropology is common, ishmaels,—as well as the difference. From the man-eating tragedy, as you have with what truth exposed it, Melville turned away, you back. I can do neither. For I remember Orpheus. . . .
>
> Nor should I be surprised if I were not a friend in your mode to H[erman] M[elville] were he alive. For I should have been impatient with him too. Men's egos are competitive, no? I also have a deep and persistent feeling: that you are too pious, that you too would have left him dry. . . .
>
> I so value your perception, your praise is a delight to me. And I would register your critique more if you did not hang it on behaviour. Again you take a high tone about something you know nothing of, Washington, Quote me Adams, Thoreau, Christ, and the labors of Hercules, all to prove I punish my own nature, endanger the fragile quiddity—the vestal fires. It is automatic of you. "Washington," "politicians," "the world," and you're off. Actually the facts are quiet. They mock you, your boobs and Barrabasses. They are yours: you dream them up.
>
> But you come up head first. Agreed: A man gets little, has little. I don't know that I want to be like Buddha and the Cow when I am a blood-letter and a Bull, but you are right about the end. And I would condition it, as you have, "if you are fortunate," though I do not threaten myself when I add it. But there, we invoke different gods.[46]

Since the two men parted company in 1941, they had taken a number of shared assumptions in very different directions, in their writings and in their lives. A brief look at the years Olson was away from Dahlberg reveals the divergence in the courses each had set for himself.

*   *   *

After quarreling with Dahlberg, Olson stopped writing. Unlike Dahlberg, though, Olson did not cloister himself away from a world now in turmoil. During World War II he remained in New York, deferred from military service because he was the sole support of his mother. He held several jobs that were tangentially related to the kind of "work" he was, at this time, most at home with. From May to July of 1941 he was the Publicity Director for the American Civil Liberties Union. From November of 1941 to August 1941, he was "Chief of the Foreign Language Information Service, Common

82

Council for American Unity" where he was responsible for collating and editing translations and summaries of stories from foreign language newspapers in America.[37]

In September of 1942, he moved to Washington with his wife, Constance Wilcock (whom he had met in New York in 1940), to take on the job of "Associate Chief, Foreign Language Division" in the Office of War Information. Olson remained in Washington for the next few years, becoming more involved in politics. He resigned his job with the O.W.L. in May of 1944 and became the director of the Foreign Nationalities Division of the Democratic Party's National Committee.

The facts about Olson's political career are not very clear, but it does seem that he did not become popular or politically powerful enough with the Democratic officials to be offered the more substantial posts that he may have been considered for—Assistant Secretary of the Treasury and, ironically (given his father's fight with Postal authorities), the office of Postmaster General. It is not certain exactly what caused Olson to leave national politics and the Democratic Party. One guess is growing outrage with what he witnessed of the backroom tactics of party officials. Whatever the reasons, Olson "officially" resigned in 1945 while spending the winter in Key West, Florida, where the Party had its winter quarters.

During the winter of 1945, Olson began writing poetry. And, when he returned to Washington on April 13 and learned that Roosevelt had died, he "started Ishmael that afternoon, the afternoon [he] kissed off [his] political future."[38] A combination of forces, as Olson would have it, also made this the right moment for returning to the Melville work. To Ann Charters he recalled having composed the book in

> one piece, and . . . written at a clip starting April 13th 1945, and finished before the 1st A-bomb, 1st week in August that same year . . . no connection to the ms. of 1940 at all. And in the interim—until April 13th, '45, I had been wholly absorbed in Foreign Nationality business & politics. (Actually, until November, 1944, or rightly date Jan. 1st, 1945, when I set in Key West, to write like forever![39]

Though Olson claimed "no connection to the ms. of 1940 at all," there certainly was a connection to "Lear and Moby-Dick," which Olson reworked and included in *Call Me Ishmael*.

Though the influence of Shakespeare on Melville commands a central position in the book, Olson modified his sense of its importance over the intervening years. The Shakespearean influence on *Moby-Dick* now became a part of a larger interpretation of Melville. "Put it this way," Olson wrote. "Three forces operated to bring about the dimensions of *Moby-Dick*: Melville, a man of MYTH, antemosaic; an experience of SPACE, its power and price, America; and ancient magnitudes of TRAGEDY, Shakespeare."[40] Olson's style is refreshing after the self-conscious attempt to imitate Dahlberg in the earlier version of the Melville study. The book was both a stylistic and conceptual breakthrough for him. With the impact of Dahlberg's lessons now assimilated, Olson could give free rein to his subjective impulses and take the necessary risks involved in sounding one's "voice." For the most part, Olson abandoned the complex allusiveness of Dahlberg's style for one that transferred his own, natural speaking tones: clipped, colloquial, emphatic. Olson's intellectual discoveries and syntheses are delivered to the reader with the same excitement and exuberance these perceptions held for him. Take, for instance, Olson's summary statement about the Melville-Shakespeare connection:

> It has to do with size, and how you value it. You can approach BIG America and spread yourself like a pancake, sing her stretch as Whitman did, be puffed up as we are over PRODUCTION. It's easy. THE AMERICAN WAY. Soft. Turns out paper cups, lies flat on the brush. N. G. . . .
> Or you can take an attitude, the creative vantage. See her as OBJECT in MOTION, something to be shaped, for use. It involves a first act of physics. You can observe POTENTIAL and VELOCITY separately, have to, to measure THE THING. You get approximate results. . . .
> Melville did his job. He calculated, and cast Ahab. BIG, first of all. ENERGY, next. PURPOSE: lordship over nature. SPEED: of the brain. DIRECTION: vengeance. COST: the people, the Crew.
> Ahab is FACT, the Crew the IDEA. The Crew is where what America stands for got into *Moby-Dick*. They're what we imagine stands for got into *Moby-Dick*. They're what we imagine democracy to be. They're Melville's addition to tragedy as he took it from Shakespeare.[41]

New interests flooded the Melville study in its reshaped form. Olson included concepts from physics; his economic critique of the importance of the whaling industry as a parallel to modern capitalism; and the historical documents narrating the wreck of the whaleship Essex, which Olson had uncovered and retells at the opening of the book in order to place Melville's work in its "man-eating" context. These and other elements were part of the intellectual ferment that was struggling for release in the book, despite the cost in placid, logical exposition. Olson's vision of the complexity of Melville's range of concerns in the novel often issues in an eliptical, almost shorthand manner. One reviewer, Lewis Mumford, took a rather sour view of *Call Me Ishmael*. For him, Olson was not enough the scholar or the dialectician, and he rather flatly characterized the book: "The work follows the intuitive line of D. H. Lawrence and Edward Dahlberg, and the reader is forced to take or leave Mr. Olson's thesis without benefit of persuasion or scholarly argument."[42]

Olson's thesis was that Melville, in his reshaping of historical events regarding the whaling industry, had explored an American myth, Space, and man's attempt to master it through the control of nature and social economics. The tragic dimensions of *Moby-Dick* had overwhelmed Melville, Olson argued, and for the rest of his life he searched for a faith that could rescue him from his despair. Melville had opened himself to life-long, nihilistic doubt through the mercilessness of the struggle he portrayed in *Moby-Dick*. Olson traced Melville's initial gropings with Shakespeare as a possible source of wisdom and thus intellectual solace, Melville's later reaching out to Christ for belief, and his search for ultimate answers in the civilization and mythologies of the ancient world. The book's scholarship had been assiduously done: Olson went through the Melville family papers and knew, intimately, the facts of Melville's despairing quest for meaning. But Olson chose not to write an academic study.

Instead, his concern was indeed subjective, assertive, proclamatory. He had learned from Dahlberg that criticism was an expression of the imagination, and this personal vision dominated the tone of the book. As in "Lear and Moby-Dick," Olson asks us to read Melville's *Journal Up the Straits*, an autobiographical record of his mounting disillusionment written in 1856 on a journey to the Holy Land, and to participate in a re-enactment of the events through Olson's skillful handling of the narrative facts.

> Two weeks in the Holyland sealed Melville in a bitterness of disillusion from which he never recovered, out of which, fifteen years later, he wrote *Clarel*, that rosary of doubt.... The stones, the rubble in the pool of Bethesda, Sodom's "bitumen & ashes," the Dead Sea with the foam on its beach "like slaver of mad dog," and the Holy Sepulcher "a sickening cheat" led Melville to one final question:
>
>> Is the desolation of the land the result of the fatal embrace of the Deity?
>
> Melville became Christ's victim, and it was death, and lack of love, let him be it. "Poor soul, the centre of my sinful earth," Shakespeare wrote. Melville became unsure of the center. It had been strong, a backward and downward in him like Ahab's.... He denied himself in Christianity. It is space, and its feeding on man, that is the essence of his vision, bred in him here in America, and it is time which is at the heart of Christianity. What the Pacific had confirmed for him he allowed Christ to undo. It was on the promise of a future life that Melville caught.
>
> Death bothered him. That bare-headed life under the grass, his own, worried him, in Dickinson's words, like a wasp. He looked for solace to

85

the Resurrection. He got nothing. For the loss of mortality he got nothing in return. The dimensions of life as he had felt them merely dwindled. Objects lose their gravity as they bulk in space.

All he has left in 1856 in the shell of his own faith: he tells Hawthorne he has "pretty much made up his mind to be annihilated."[43]

We can see throughout the book how Olson wished to free his discussion of a subtle, psychological state from the "objective" trappings of customary scholarship. He sought to dramatize these psychic forces so that the reader could experience them directly—without elaboration or reservation.

The historical and biographical facts surrounding Melville's life and times form the structure of the book, beginning with Olson's recounting of the wreck of the *Essex*, the historical counterpart of the *Pequod*, and ending with his historical context—specifically, that of America's nineteenth-century expansion westward. Olson discovered in Melville a myth-maker as powerful as Homer or Dante:

> At the end of the *Paradiso*, when from the seventh sphere the earth is so small its features are obscured as the moon's to us, Dante recognizes one spot on all its surface—that entrance to the West, the Pillars. Dante's last glance is on the threshold to that future Columbus made possible.
>
> The third and final odyssey was Ahab's. The Atlantic crossed, the new land America known, the dream's death lay around the Horn, where West returned to East. The Pacific is the end of the UNKNOWN which Homer's and Dante's Ulysses opened men's eyes to. END of individual responsible only to himself. Ahab is full stop.[44]

Here, and throughout the book, in contrast to Dahlberg's highly wrought, archaic style, Olson's prose is terse, muscular. But the variety of rhythms in his sentences, their evocative flavor, their reliance on the individualistic tone —all suggest Dahlberg's guiding impulse.

During their years apart, Olson reflected on the relevance of a historical context with regard to Melville and his major novel. Olson pursued history as a source of creative inspiration for the remainder of his life. He gave numerous talks, wrote and lectured on the need for an awareness of history as an indispensible tool in aiding man to understand himself, his origins, and ultimately his own soul. Olson's youthful fascination with history matured in *Call Me Ishmael*. Yet his interest, unlike Dahlberg's, lay not with history and the literature of the past as a kind of storehouse of apothogems, maxims, and isolate myths. Nor did Olson go to the past to "check" his style. Rather, Olson identified history as a state of consciousness that ultimately reconnected man with his ancestors of the world.

Olson began to visit Ezra Pound at St. Elizabeth's Hospital in Washington in January of 1946. By this time, he had finished *Call Me Ishmael* and was looking for a publisher. Pound read the manuscript, thought well of it, and referred it to T. S. Eliot who was an editor for Faber & Faber. Eliot turned the manuscript down, but Olson managed to place it with Reynal and Hitchcock, who published it early in 1947. Both Pound and William Carlos Williams further strengthened Olson's sense of history's importance, especially in poetry. The two older men had already developed open forms to accommodate both their personal and historical concerns. Most probably their double influence caused Olson's later change of direction toward poetry as the major creative outlet in his life. Both Williams and Pound later met with Dahlberg's sour disapproval, and he let Olson know how much he disliked both and the influences they were then exerting on Olson's work. Pound was, for Dahlberg, "the artistic mountebank who puts Topeka and Telemachus together to make a canto";[45] Williams, whom Dahlberg knew, was simply "the baby doctor with the obituary satchel of pills."[46]

Initially, Olson intended to cover Pound's sanity trial for *Twice-A-Year*. He wrote to Dorothy Norman stating that purpose. She was extremely interested in the project, but Olson never submitted any of his extensive notes. Pound's and Olson's was a quiet relationship in which Olson could feel at ease, unlike the earlier skirmishes with Dahlberg. Before *Call Me Ishmael* was published and Dahlberg renewed their friendship, Olson wrote, with regard to Pound as well as Dahlberg:

> I wish only to offer him some personal comforts, do some chores for him like getting people to write to him, and give him an ear more or less able to be sympathetic. And this, for the work he has done. And what I now feel, the charm and attraction of his person. For he is handsome and quick and at work as ever. His jumps in conversation are no more than I or any active mind would make. Once in awhile he seems to speak with an obsession, but even this I do, and at this age, after the fullness of his life, I imagine I might be a hell of a lot worse. I think of Dahlberg already.[47]

Despite their break, the intellectual presence of Dahlberg had not left Olson. Olson worked with Dahlberg's notes during the composition of *Call Me Ishmael*. He recopied Dahlberg's marginilia into one of his working journals during the book's writing. Olson simply lists Dahlberg's comments about those 1940 drafts in the notebook without explanation. Without exception they expressed Dahlberg's belief that Olson needed to direct his writing inward, to "feel" his ideas and his language:

> Exteriorized—not myths imagined in the pool of *your own blood stream*
>
> be wary of definitions—write a mythic sentence out of which *your "super-stition"* arises

be, in your prose, one of those *mysteries*

all this cosmology not internal, not mired in *your own identity*

... from which ideas + feelings do not *issue*
... does not issue *as parable*
... not *uttered out of your self*
... all this, so fine, is technical, explorative rather than *human fable*
... nothing *felt* all *outside*[48]

In the same notebook Olson also sketched an inscription for a presentation copy of *Call Me Ishmael* to Dahlberg. The copy and the inscription were never sent. At the time, though, Olson acknowledged, if only privately, the significance of Dahlberg to the book. He wrote:

For him who was my Corinth, and brought this book to be

EDWARD DAHLBERG

I send you, with the greatest joy, the very first copy of a book which you as I acknowledge [broken off]

Beyond all others I took life from you and shall give it back as long as I write.

I have one hope—that you will find the book the Sphinx you demanded. In any case what you demanded has always been my guide and goal.[49]

And there were other meditations like the following, written in Florida, before Olson returned to Washington and began the sprint of work that resulted in *Call Me Ishmael.*

My spirit, like my body and my potency, is fragile. I do not think any of them shall continue so but in this passage of life, this phase of the moon, it is so. C makes firm my genitals, the South could strengthen my muscles, and life will toughen my spirit. They all become fragile when my faith in myself is low flame. How to have faith. How to assume the illusion of one's self! And it is hardest with the spirit.

What regimen can I give my spirit? A quickening of instant consciousness is obvious need. But something in me resists such concentration. I wonder if that something is not weak and bad, an indulgence, a sentimentality. On the other hand, consciousness with me passes too quickly into intelligence, and the intelligence is despair. The mind is a cynic, passive and offensively detached. The Gilgamesh in my heart is in my head God and bad. ... Only after my heart has brooded long does my head have the right to lead. But my head is quicker than my heart. How to learn to insist always only so far as my heart has gone. But my heart may well have gone that far, and yet be unknown. That's where writing strengthens, only as poet. And as poet in scale. All these lyrics you are writing are nice, but dangerous. Leap ahead and try the ambitions. Go to the extreme of your imagination and go on from there: fail large, never succeed small. Again ED[ahlberg] makes sense: one intuition must only lead to another farther place.[50]

In "Projective Verse," an essay published in 1950, Olson returned to this principle from Dahlberg, crediting him in the text with the idea. Olson transformed Dahlberg's words on imaginative risk-taking into a formula for accelerating composition and thus outdistancing "ennui." The result was the often quoted rule of "Projective Verse":

> ... ONE PERCEPTION MUST IMMEDIATELY AND DIRECTLY LEAD TO A FURTHER PERCEPTION. It means exactly what it says, is a matter of, at *all* points (even, I should say, of our management of daily reality as of the daily work) get on with it, keep moving, keep in, speed, the nerves, their speed, the perceptions, theirs, the acts, the split second acts, the whole business, keep it moving as fast as you can, citizen. And if you also set up as a poet, USE USE USE the process at all points, in any given poem always, always one perception must must must MOVE INSTANTER, ON ANOTHER![51]

It should be remembered that the learning of how to write from "the pulse" was to be the crucial entrance for Olson in his development as a writer. The emphasis on the oral, and, by extension, the physical qualities of language became a dominating feature of the poetry Olson wrote in the last twenty years of his life. In the course of his work on *Call Me Ishmael* and his beginning to write poetry, the lessons from Dahlberg coalesced with the newer influences of Williams and Pound. Both of the latter would further commit his writing to the reliance on the organic sources of language, with the measure of the written word's veracity relying on its adherence to the emotions that are its causes. But Olson's readiness for Pound and Williams would not have been so telling were it not for the earlier impact of Dahlberg.

Even before his realignment with Dahlberg, Olson's sights were on poetry. What seems to be implicit in the passage from Florida quoted above is Olson's attraction toward the longer, more "ambitious" forms of Pound in *The Cantos* and, later, Williams in *Paterson*. What is more important, perhaps, is Olson's conviction that he must return to writing. The period of contact with "the world" and the years of gestation were giving way, around 1945, to the desire for further creative production.

Olson dedicated the chapter on Christ in *Call Me Ishmael* to Dahlberg. Apparently Olson's "heart" and "head" were not in accord on the matter of sending the copy with the warm, personal inscription. Thus, he opened himself to Dahlberg's charges of his being "clandestine" about the book and Dahlberg's influences upon it. Dahlberg's point about Olson's lack of courtesy is not distorted. The published dedication bears out the ambiguity Olson attached to their strained relationship. No wonder Dahlberg found it loaded and, from his point of view, cutting. It was addressed to

EDWARD DAHLBERG, my other genius of the Cross and the Windmills. If the Fool is in this book, you nurtured him.

Melville read Don Quixote as you have. He did it at a most important time, when he was turning for succor, as I imagine you have turned, to the Mediterranean world, and Christ. He acquired his copy in September 1855.

Two of the passages he marked belong to your experience as to his. I want you particularly to have them.

Sancho Panza alone believed all that his master said to be true, knowing who he was, and having been acquainted with him from his birth.

The other is Don Antonio's cry against all the Simon Carrascos of life who gloat when they have unseated a poor Knight:

Oh! sir, God forgive you the injury you have done the whole world, in endeavouring to restore to his senses the most diverting madman in it.

With friendship resumed after the publication of *Call Me Ishmael*, Olson eventually sent Dahlberg an inscribed copy of the book. Aware of Dahlberg's suspicious reading of the dedication and of his demand for fuller recognition, Olson rekindled the personal tribute he had originally meant but ultimately had hesitated to commit himself to. This time he called Dahlberg "the begetter" of the work and sent with that acknowledgement "[his] love" and "the lines of Ben Jonson from his epigram to his great master: Camden! most revered head, to whom I owe all that I am in arts, all that I know."[52]

CHAPTER SIX

Ultimate "Divergencies"

You are the only man in the world with whom I have had misunderstandings ... and they arose precisely because, with you, I did not want to remain
within the limits of a simple friendship. I wanted to go further and deeper.
But I plunged ahead recklessly, collided with you and upset you and then,
seeing my error, drew back, too suddenly perhaps. And that is why a
"breach" grew up between us. Then, too, I am much older than you. I have
followed a different path. . . . Your whole life is facing forward, mine is built
on the past. . . . You are too solidly planted on your own feet to become a
disciple of anything! I can assure you that I never thought you were ma-
licious or dreamed you were capable of literary jealousy. I saw in you
(forgive the expression!) a considerable amount of confusion, but never anything evil. And you are far too perceptive not to know that if either of us
has anything to envy the other, you are surely not the one. In a word, we
will never be friends in Rousseau's sense, but we will love each other and
rejoice in each other's success and, after you have settled down and all that
is surging around inside you has subsided a little, then, I am certain of it,
we shall meet again as joyfully and openly as on the day I met you for the
first time. . . . —TURGENEV to TOLSTOY, September 13, 1856

During the late 1940's, Olson was beginning to channel more and more of
his creative energies into poetry. And while Dahlberg did not care for the
new influences on Olson's work (Pound and Williams), he nonetheless continued to be one to whom Olson sent most of his finished work. Dahlberg,
too, once more sought Olson's advice about a manuscript he had completed
in August of 1948.

Dahlberg called the work an "autobiography," but the characters and
situations were partially fictionalized. At a later date he characterized it as
"part fable and part essay." He titled the manuscript, *The Flea of Sodom.*
Its mode was allegorical and satiric, treating Dahlberg's experiences in the
Communist circles of New York in the 1930's. The setting of the narrative
portion of the piece is an apocalyptical, modern city that, like Sodom, has
collapsed into perversity and moral chaos. The place is peopled by a bizarre
mélange of ancient, mythological figures whom Dahlberg makes contemporary—Monsieur Golem Patron, Pilate Agenda, Ephraim Bedlam, Andro-
mache Lucy, Thais Collette. The story is episodic, picaresque. All is deca-

dence; moral and ethical meaning has become absurd, Party-line jargon. Real personages are converted into grotesques. Throughout the work and amid the inane cavortings of the Communist crowd, moments of clear sanity break through. Dahlberg's prophetic voice intones against the senselessness, juxtaposing modern insanity with ancient and proverbial "wisdom":

> The Myth cannot ripen where the olive does not grow. Men abhor the gods, the houses are Satan's bile, the ground, infernal asphalt of Gorgon Medusa. The harpies have bedunged the streets and victuals because the Oracles have been forsaken for Progress which is sloth. This Atlantic non-entity, muttering Babel's homogeneous words, hatches his slovenly cities anywhere. All his inventions are for his piggish apathy. He travels in the machines to remote places to shake his bowels. Bothering little with man-ual arts his hands are so testy that he commits crimes to handle a tool! Cyclops dungs more privily than he who lives in a house on the highway for the companionship of tin automobiles. He furtively diets on prurient newspaper pictures of female legs until he has the priapic fit, and loses his seed in Onan's cinema pit.[1]

Along with "The Flea of Sodom," Dahlberg included another piece, "The Rational Tree," a testament of his belief in the relevance of the past to the present, grafted from his studies of the ancient writers that drew most of his intellectual attention during his isolation of the early forties, just after he and Olson had broken contact. He enclosed both works with further remarks about his friendship with Olson and his feeling about his role in the relationship:

> I always wanted you to understand that I was never in competition with you, not because I am so sure of myself. Nothing could be less true of my own pulses. All I care about is to utter some Edenic Truths, and perhaps either in dream or in trance to lower my eyes as Helen descends the steps or to bow my face to the ground as Abraham did when God spoke to him.
>   People have said I have deeply influenced you. This is a foolish remark. Of course, I probably have, and that is why you wrote as you did, very beautiful, murmuring sea lines, and not as I could. There can be no literature without a small tender group of men of feeling who are con-stantly sharpening each other. What people who do not understand such a simple truth as this is miss is that I could not have written CALL ME ISHMAEL, or even one lovely line in it.
>   If we are to continue in our friendship, and I wish it for my sake and also deeply for yours, not because I deem myself a purer imagination than yours, but because you require my guidance.[2]

Olson responded more favorably to "The Rational Tree" section and per-suaded Dahlberg to make a clearer separation between "The Flea" and this "Book of Edverbs, the Mount of Dahl," as he styled the piece. He went on:

"It is wise as men are not. It is apothegm, uttered, uddered, and thrusts, from your appetence." After further editorial suggestions and a promsie to do whatever he could to help get the book into print, Olson hurried, he said, "to put into [his] blood" the "sayings" of the work.[3]

Olson was again actively gathering material for his own work from Dahlberg. For example, a passage from "The Rational Tree" impressed Olson very much, and he assimilated the "sayings" the passage held for him. Dahlberg had exhorted the virtues of the sedentary, meditative life and gave Olson the beginning for a poem, later called, "Tyrian Business" in *The Maximus Poems* (1960). In his passage Dahlberg had concluded that "the seer was he who sat." He went on to invoke a pastoral, Biblical sense of calm, curbing his drives into an acceptance of the sedentary fate of the writer and the conditions of his own life:

> Man knows no more evil stroke than to walk to and fro in the earth as Lucifer does, and has no other balm for the pain in his spirit than to be still. Be quiet, my ribs; stay home, lambs and goats of Ai. Rest; the ships of Tarsish are in your room: Eden is in a chair. Sit, my heart, and Schechem and Uz are thine.[4]

When Olson reshaped the idea, his more expansive, physical concerns pronounced themselves:

> 1
>
> The waist of a lion,
> for a man to move properly
>
> And for a woman,
> who should move lazily,
> the weight of breasts
> This is the exercise for this morning
>
> 2
>
> how to dance
> sitting down[5]

Later in the poem, Olson transformed another section from "The Rational Tree" into an obscure allusion. Dahlberg wrote:

> Golgotha's nails punish the spirit no more than a hamlet or city that has nothing left of the holy footprints of Elijah but the crop of gravel Virgil cast down the three throats of Cerberus. The face is hindered and the navel sickened in abominable places. It was a soul in its nauseous moan that chided the twelve disciples for exclaiming, 'What a stench!', when passing dog-carrion, by replying, 'How white the teeth are!' Had not Jesus, who doted on the albic stole and the frankincense, been reared in

93

Galilee whose twenty foul towns Solomon had guilefully presented to Hiram of Tyre?[6]

As before, Olson fragmented and personalized the incident, making of it a kind of private aside. Dahlberg's apocryphal tale is didactic in so far as it adds to our sense of Christ. Olson's use of the same material is not interested in the content of the tale, but rather in its mysterious, evocative power. It is tucked away against the left margin of the page, while the rest of Olson's poem leads the eye to the lower right-hand corner:

> He sd: Notice
> the whiteness, not
> the odor of
> the dead night

Other allusions in Olson's poems and prose can be traced to the exchanges between Olson and Dahlberg. On the whole, they are, for Olson, acts of remembering and thus naturally work themselves into the poems, in which Olson means to reflect the process of the poet's mind. But for the reader unfamiliar with both men's work, they are often elliptical, esoteric, puzzling. Even after Olson moved permanently away from Dahlberg in the 1950's and explored for himself the open forms of Williams and Pound, there are numerous tonal qualities and subjects that continue to suggest the lingering presence of Dahlberg.

Olson's poetry upset Dahlberg. After they had quarreled again and parted for good, he would call it "refrigerated verse." But as early as 1953 he was remarking to a friend that Olson was "writing verse that Thoth, the goddess of the alphabet, could not comprehend."[7] During the late 1940's Dahlberg was patient, if not entirely receptive to Olson's new poetic enthusiasm and the influences of Pound and Williams that Olson was reflecting in his verse. Dahlberg objected primarily to Olson's lack of "the darkling speaking heart" in the poems he had asked Dahlberg to read and comment on. In 1948, Olson published a group of poems, *Y & X*, and sent the small book to Dahlberg. In one of the poems Olson alluded to the Nazi atrocities of the recent war, and Dahlberg used the reference as a jumping-off point for a larger criticism of the poetry.

> There is only one jot of dross in all the verses. You will find no healing seaweed or salts in a Buchenwald. You are too abstruse to require *more* experience. Vent your Angers, and the Muses will give you fillets and sweet calamus.

He used the rest of the letter as an occasion to placate Olson, to assure him of his abiding friendship, and to once more urge him to return to the ancient themes Dahlberg himself found so necessary to his own work:

> Please do not be vexed with me. No man is a more steadfast Horatio to your Genius than I am, but I look for the crowing of the dawn in your nature, for the Morning Star, Lucifer, to make its his, and I want to see the piteous Ghost that wails so secretly, and in the nightside of ourselves, drop its filmy garment upon the head, and then disappears as one man vanishes from another after he has emitted the nether deposits of his identity.

He reflected on himself, Ishmael:

> At the moment, I am a nullity, and hear nothing but the song of the Worms.

The closing was firm, however, and meant to encourage:

> Do not think that I do not consider these poems of dear Worth, or that I go hankering after some churl of letters for better ones. They are the best, but they are not good enough for me from Charles Olson.[8]

The difficulty in Dahlberg's equivocal appreciation of the poems lay in his tremendous dislike of Pound and the effects he felt Pound was having on Olson. He could tolerate neither Pound's anti-Semitism nor his creative "originality." In a later letter to Olson Dahlberg frankly stated his feelings: "The only proposition I would earnestly ask you to ponder, or to dismiss is this: the difference between CALL ME ISHMAEL and Y & X is the ultimate distinction between Edward Dahlberg and Ezra Pound."[9]

Other letters between them pursued the subject of Olson's poetry, with Dahlberg always asking for less obscurity, less colloquial and vernacular language, and for more reliance on the Old Testament and the Homeric Greeks, for examples, for themes and language, for wisdom and truth. In "Bellerophon," a section of *The Flea of Sodom* (finally published in England in 1950), Dahlberg attempted to embody Olson in the mythological character and thus speak to him about the nature of poetry.

> If a poem does not make the spirit shake as the reed in the wind, it is for infidel unfaith, for Pride, and if a man has not learned from heaven that verse is made in unclean tombs or at Cana, then let God write the BOOK, and men go down in the dust to read it.[10]

The treatment of Olson in "Bellerophon" allowed Dahlberg to explain Olson the poet and Olson the man in a detached manner. His complaint against Olson was that he possessed too much knowledge and too little heartfelt wisdom. It was meant to stand as an admonition and an omen, as well as a criticism. In it, we hear once again Dahlberg's aversions to Olson's experiments in poetry:

> Bellerphon sued the Winds for feral privacies; but writing, like dying, is a private act, the ritual of the soul in its descent to Styx and the Dream. It is the dying for new forms, the expiratory pang of Orpheus for Eurydice in Hades. The Orphic poet must return as quickly as he can to sane, dry light, for though the Dream writes everything, it is the NEGATIVE ANGEL of the LIVING WILL. Space, shoreless, inward God, and the surging, evening images of Pathless Dream, produce in men, whose will has been relaxed by watery Tartarus, jibing OWL'D ANGELS of Reason.[11]

Of Bellerophon/Olson he demanded contact, human, "MORTAL TOUCH" —"the parent of all literature"—as opposed to the "Cyclopic iron Mountains of the intellectual faculties." As Bellerophon, he urged Olson to question:

> What is the mind that it should bray, or go proud and alone? Genius is a sacred Animal that trembles more than others and requires an Archangel to prevent him from wearing out his heart for human sorrow. Return to the fig-trees beneath the walls of Ilium to chant to the timourous, dove-winged mind. Go low, Bellerophon, come down, O learned Dust, Wisdom is our PRAYER.

Dahlberg (who must be seen here as the "Arch-angel") conveys a sense of Olson that Olson himself confirms and may even have spoken to Dahlberg about—that need to know his own heart to the full before reaching out for intellectual conclusions.

Olson was so taken by Dahlberg's portrait of him and by the book as a whole that he wrote Dahlberg proposing that he do a "critique" of it. During the summer of 1950, Olson wrote several long letters to Dahlberg in response to the Bellerophon section and repeated his intent to review the book. But other commitments interrupted Olson's working on the study.

Since the fall of 1948, Olson had been teaching at Black Mountain College in North Carolina. He took over a position that Dahlberg had held briefly and quickly resigned, having recommended Olson as his replacement. Dahlberg stayed at the college for a few weeks and then left in a huff, disenchanted with the country setting and the students.[12] Olson, at Dahlberg's insistence, took the vacant post, dividing his time between Washington and Black Mountain, between his own writing and the new demands of teaching. Olson was also busy with other commitments. He gave several public readings and lectures during 1948, 1949, and 1950. In 1948 he applied for and received another Guggenheim fellowship to work on a book about the relationship between the American Indian, the Negro, and the frontiersman.

Black Mountain affected Olson very differently than it had Dahlberg. Though the pace was often hectic during these years, Olson was excited by the energy of the place and the people it held: Merce Cunningham, Franz Kline, Joseph Albers, Buckminster Fuller, and others. Here things began to fall into place, and Olson's natural fascination with history led him into archeology and geology. But, as always seemed to be the case with Olson, one thing led to another, and he was soon intensely interested in physics and dance, modern painting and music, geometry and mathematics. It was a period of surging energy and discovery for Olson, and it would be easy to justify Olson's inability to complete the piece on *The Flea of Sodom* on the grounds of engagement in so many activities. Yet Olson had made lengthy notes toward the essay and qualified his intentions to Dahlberg. He did not wish to simply do a review of the book. Instead, he claimed to his friend, "I should want to say nothing of Edward Dahlberg which did not stand in the same mortice as the thing I might say of Herman Melville. For Edward Dahlberg is more than my friend: he is of my own substance, a personage of my own fable, and I heave him out with the gravest torment, as if it were parts of my own flesh."[13]

However, Dahlberg was anxious to have attention drawn to his book. He had divorced wife, Winifred, a few years earlier. The divorce settlements drained funds and energies. He taught Freshman Composition part-time at Brooklyn Polytechnical Institute, where he was a colleague and friend of Louis Zukovsky. The American edition of *The Flea of Sodom* was due to be published in the fall of 1950 by New Directions. Dahlberg's side of the correspondence has not survived, but one can surmise from Olson's replies to his letters that Dahlberg was insisting that Olson apply himself at once to the article on *The Flea*. As Olson put it, he recognized that Dahlberg wanted "a big-time notice for leverage on the akademicians, that time is important."[14] But Olson would not be hurried. When Olson balked at giving the piece his immediate attention, Dahlberg repeated, as he had done several years earlier, the list of obligations Olson had built up in their friendship. Olson replied to one of Dahlberg's chiding letters:

> I say, I don't know, simply because it is much more intricate than this given event. That is, you do pitch writing into love (friendship). And so a "statement", as they call it, not done, becomes, for you, a denial of *you* —not, as it would appear to me, a denial of a "system" which I think it is of some moment to keep clear of. (You will imagine I have acted likewise, did, in fact, same publisher, like problem, same time, as of

97

FLEA.) But there we are: this does not seem to you either of any moment or but more proof of yr case against me: that I am inhuman and cold and unyielding and act without those Mediterranean parts of the human body which you feel you do possess. For you wld take it, as you so warmly put it—and I am made happy by—I am yr first friend. And should act a way you declare.[15]

They disputed most of the fall of 1950. Dahlberg interpreted Olson's failure to undertake the esay as a betrayal of their friendship. Olson regarded the wrangling as another attempt by Dahlberg to manipulate the terms of the friendship. Olson told Dahlberg he did not wish to rush the work. But Dahlberg held his reluctance as a conspiracy on Olson's part to cloak his debts. Olson answered the charge that he had been "privy" in acknowledging Dahlberg's influence:

(I must, here, vent my full rejection of yr whole notion that the "privy" is what you are getting. (I completely abhor your indelicacy, in using such a word, as of myself, or anyone. Indelicacy, hell. Just straight on, known to yrself or otherwise, these adjectives—these moral adjectives: yr letter is loaded with em.) That I do not express my affection & friendship as you might, is *this* cause for you to sit in judgement on my whole nature? Was it "privy" of me to join you, in ISHMAEL, to my two other loves, to say, this was the man who, by his friendship (belief) and his "critique" of my work, put an element, Fool, here, in this book, which I would wish *anyone*, reading it, to recognize, as his doing?[16]

In writing about *The Flea of Sodom*, Olson found himself up against the enormous task of trying to "grapple with . . . the relevance of the whole of Dahlberg's vision."[17] The book "came to hand," he told Dahlberg, "at the moment that I am ready to engage them, not, as a passing act, not as another book, but as, the vision of a man who has been my mentor. (In such circumstance, there is bound to be trouble. Only, abide, dear friend," he asked Dahlberg. "You, your work, this life, is worth it.)"[18] Olson closed the letter by further defending his decision to proceed more deliberately with the study of Dahlberg vis-a-vis *The Flea of Sodom*. Here, his remarks reveal Olson's concern for the project; and in closing, refers to the burden Dahlberg had once again assigned to the friendship:

ONE   I take you very seriously   TWO   I take the art of writing very seriously   THREE   I take it, that books are men, and not to be toyed with, that there is value, which each man must go and find out.   FOUR I am engaged with setting down, what value you have.
                                                    In such circumstance
the question is huge.
    Anyhow, I wish the hell you'd sat on yr hands. But you didn't. So there it is. Let's carry it, lightly.

98

At this point Dahlberg let the matter of the study rest. There was another silence between the two men for nearly a year. Olson was away in Yucatan, studying the Mayans and continuing a series of letters to Robert Creeley, later edited by Creeley as *The Mayan Letters* (1954). "Projective Verse" appeared in *Poetry New York* in 1950. While in Mexico Olson also carried on a lengthy correspondence with Cid Corman, who was planning his magazine, *Origin*, which featured Olson in its first issue. The correspondence to Corman was also later published as a book, *Letters for Origin* (1970). Thus, Olson was riding the crest of this new wave of productivity during these few years (1950-1951), and this left little room for any kind of study of Dahlberg and *The Flea of Sodom*.

Meanwhile, Dahlberg wrote a review of Newton Arvin's book, *Herman Melville*, in which he demonstrated that Arvin had plagiarized from *Call Me Ishmael*.[19] Olson received the essay when he returned to the States. This time he was ecstatic and wrote Dahlberg first to say,

> by god, i say, to be there, in the public print, put there by you so tellingly: thank you, Edward, for the long arm of your mind & its attentions!

Olson signed the letter "with old & new love, & new thanks that you are more alert than others."[20]

Dahlberg's reply was quick to arrive. He explained the ramifications of the exposure of Arvin, along the way calling Olson's attention to his investment on Olson's behalf.

> The piece for the Freeman was two months labor and vexation. One glance at the sodomite book was enough, but to nail him on a thieve's cross at Calvary was another matter. It is done, and now your work cannot be gainsaid or garbled or pilfered. I took pains to see that no less than twenty copies went to Smith College. I know the little academic gnome was bitterly stung; everybody who has read it has said that there was no doubt that I proved that he was a robber.... Well, can you believe any more that the American writer is not some Gadarene devil? But the fight, who else has bothered but me? I have had a year's battle against Mark Van Doren, the canary Trilling up at Columbia, the albino Fitzgerald beadles, the herd academic deacons of grammar, and for what purpose? If a few would use a pen as a whip they would go to their riggish kennels, but no one will help me....
>
> I write you a little this time, Charles, but do not believe this reply is meant to be low-hearted. I wish you would do one thing, go back over the scroll of your life as a writer, and ask your own heart whether anybody has ever been so steadfast to your nature as one Edward Dahlberg, and ask what he has reaped in return, save the only knowledge that keeps him alive, and that he has always tried to tell the truth which people nowadays miscall by the name of slander and malice. Granville Hicks

wrote in a letter to Chamberlain at the Freeman, saying that he should not print Edward Dahlberg, for he was vicious and sick and that the so-called stealth from your book were coincidental, fine word, coincidental, it is so useful and marginal another word for sneaking.

Well, I too send you my love and friendship; if you know of any college that would like a composition handyman around, let me know.[21]

Olson did not reply immediately to Dahlberg's letter. After a few weeks, Dahlberg again launched an invective assault on Olson, repeating what he had done earlier after the publication of *Call Me Ishmael* and Olson's silence to his letter of praise provoked him. Again, Olson was piqued and returned the gauntlet:

i stand on my thanks to you, for LAURELS—yet i stayed silent to yr letter from Florida (rec'd last week), simply because i do not know what to do when you count coups.
the trouble is, i know & grant you the reasons of yr demarches: i know the same craving for engagement of one's force. Yet this is the double gate which won't go down. . . .

It is such a welter, these businesses between us. My silences (which you paw at) are solely I do not know what to do when the skin is the gate, when you put your armour propre on your sleeve—as though mine too were worn there. It ain't.[22]

Between 1952 and 1954 there was another break in their relationship. Olson was busy teaching at Black Mountain and working on his first group of *Maximus* poems. Dahlberg travelled a good deal, finally settling on the West Coast with his new wife RLene. He also wrote some poems and continued as a book reviewer for the *Freeman*, in which he had a regular column called "Second Harvest." He wrote reviews of Williams' *Autobiography* and Pound's *Letters*, accusing Williams of "concealment" and Pound of pretension. His interest in the sacred books of the ancient American Indians and the journals of the early explorers in this country was sparked by the review he did for the *Freeman* of Garcilaso de la Vega's *The Florida of the Inca*. The work for the *Freeman* also put him in touch with a number of biographies, ranging from Poe to Tolstoy, a mode of writing that would later mature for him in his own autobiographical works, *Because I was Flesh* (1964), and *The Confessions* (1971). It was a time for Dahlberg of an expanding inquiry into "beginnings," with regard to his early years as well as to the mythological and historical origins of various cultures.

By November of 1954, he and Olson had begun to correspond again. This time the occasion for their renewed communication was Robert Creeley, whom Olson knew from Black Mountain and whom Dahlberg met and became friendly with in Mallorca, Spain, where he vacationed in 1954. Their correspondence is fragmentary from this point to the end of their friendship in 1955. Once again, the channels of any fluid, lighter friendship were dammed by Dahlberg's bitterness. He could not forgive Olson for his failure to fulfill expectations. Olson, on the other hand, felt a constant frustration in his attempts to penetrate what he believed was Dahlberg's pose of self-righteousness and superiority. He felt thwarted each time he tried to force on Dahlberg an awareness of the "divergencies" of their personalities and lives.

The role of the dutiful son to Dahlberg's patriarchial authority chafed Olson. He could not dispel the guilt Dahlberg attached to Olson's behaviour and what Dahlberg considered Olson's "desertions" of him during the crucial moments in their relationship. For Dahlberg, their friendship was a fate. He told Olson: "You are a part of my memory and experiences, and I can brew nothing in that poor limbeck called the heart, without in some way including you, nor can you do otherwise."[23] In the same letter, Dahlberg pointedly reminded Olson of the Newton Arvin expose, again invoking the tones of the outcast Ishmael: "If I finally was driven by the dingiest political dunciads to do a column for the fetid New Freeman, I had to appear some-where, for I grow weary of putting all my work away for rust and moths and epitaphs."[24]

The issue of their latest quarrel was the influence of Pound and Williams on Olson's language and the forms of his poetry. Dahlberg believed the use of the vernacular to be a debasement, a perversity. But Olson retaliated: "You're so foolish, not to come down off the mountain and figure that some of us can be concerned without wanting a large stiff language of stones, of self-canonization."[25] But the quarrel was only symptomatic of a deeper fissure dividing the men—namely, the fact that they were in competition with each other. Olson's fortunes were on the rise, with the "Projective Verse" essay, the attention in *Origin*, and his becoming Rector of Black Mountain College. Though he never said so in so many words, Dahlberg envied the other's success. Dahlberg's defenses of his own penurious existence are made so often in these late letters and at such length that one cannot help but agree with Olson and regard them as attempted leverage to gain moral superiority in their relationship.

In terms of their intellectual interests, again both were involved with similar material. Both were delving into the lore of the early explorers in America and attempting to understand the effects of the New World on both the indigenous civilizations and the intruding mythology of the Old World. As before, without the other's knowledge, they had each come to the

101

same "wafty bridge" in the subject matter of their writing. Dahlberg sent Olson a piece he wrote on LaSalle's expedition for the magazine, *Nimbus*. Olson objected to the way Dahlberg had cast the Old World penetration into the New as a "*wrong* loaded weighing of Indians versus Jews-Greeks-Egyptians." The contention grew over how to consider the events of the European migrations to America. Olson believed the "vernacular" told the story with more "force," and he felt Dahlberg was "loading the continent as Indian versus man as ancient, and wrong[ing] the former by scoriation—and man with him—and wrong[ing] the latter by sentimentality about how human life was then."[26]

For Olson it came down to a matter of language, its ability freshly and forcefully to convey a sense of historical events. The colloquial was thus a more powerful vehicle for transmitting the harshness of the ordeal. Dahlberg disagreed vehemently, apparently, for Olson's response was pitched in anger:

> My beef here is your slamming around about the vernacular—my "abstract" vernacular, Pound's "glacial"—and who else's what vernacular (?) What's your fear, Mister Man?
> Obviously it isn't. It's that you have misled yourself about the nature of language: you think it's vocabulary. The rest of us guess it's for real. You think it's words. The rest of us think it's force. Thus you are drawn up into the head (?) (and talk so much of the viscera?) Again, I burn that you should propose some slackening of my intelligence due to some Marxian ghost which leads me to seek commerce with the people ???? wot People??? . . .
>
> There are two prongs for any man of intelligence who reads to write (so far as I know there are you and Pound and me, who else?)
> Ok. (The others have better sense. Bill, e.g., And Creeley, say). But if you are foolish (and so am I) the double prong is scholarship and vernacular, that combo. And solely for one reason: the discrete, and the continuous.[27]

Dahlberg calmly replied:

> I have found great fault with your vernacular because I do not believe it nourishes either the faculties or the fingers, the foot, the arm, or the belly. I thought your poem in the Black Mountain Review disgraceful. Why you throw off something of that sort I cannot tell, except that you must have some wanton appetite to *shit* upon yourself. . . . I lament that sort of street barbarism. I don't go to a book to find out what I already know. I know more about the language of the gamin than you, and if you doubt it, read your butchered syntax, which you imagine is the speech of the people, and then go to Bottom Dogs. But do not think that the scrabbled gutturals of an auto mechanic are as savory or have the same moral or human weight as the words of a rustic or any bumpkin living

before the machine, the cartel, and the big inhuman cities came as the black angel to every nation.

Yes, I go back to Babylon, Egypt, to the Indus, always searching for the beginnings; it will bring me much woe, and maybe, mutilate sentences. At times, I look at an improper adjective and expire in a blush. I have said many times that the writer cannot be wildly alone, and not make mistakes that a simple proof-reader could correct. The trouble is we don't even have the proof-readers any more. What with the dying out of artisanship the sentence is ill-made, or amateurish.[28]

In the margin of the letter, Olson drew a line next to the last paragraph, labelling the theme of the loss of craftsmanship and the need to return to an earlier, better time, "ever-reworked." Next to the following paragraph in the letter, Olson printed a large, "IT" in the margin, with an arrow pointing to Dahlberg's by now familiar and perhaps for Olson, obvious peroration:

I don't care for literary relations. I am a friend or I don't bother with people, and that includes you. You take on airs telling the man who reared you as a writer about having an artistic correspondence with him. That's all right for pederasts and self-seekers, but not for me. I still think, which is quite naive when I do it, but realistic when you do so, that we write books to create a polity grounded in affection. I am a portable tomb out here, and I don't need your epistles, often half-crazy, and on occasion shot through with some burning truth, to kindle the cold hearth in my soul. If I brought you into the world to be a writer now to prate to me about literary relationship, then I committed another grievous error. When you needed me, I did not say to you, you are ambitious, vain, self-loving and turn my back upon your position. No, I said to you, Charles, you are fancy, precious, a peevish Narcissus, but I will help you. This difference between us makes for literature; you imagine you are coming down to the multitude by your use of jargon which they know better than you. I am not so pretentious or mad. You feign to write for yourself alone; I say simply, but forlornly, I write, and I am alone.

You imagine that being gross is an assertion of your vitality; my reply is that it is gross to accept a kindness from a man who has been your friend for so many years without even troubling to write him even a few words of thanks. I see, you hanker after friends, too, but the young are your fancy, because they cannot find out your faults as readily as I can. It is my duty to be of help to any gifted man in this terrible voiceless wilderness. Don't make a mistake about me. I'm not on my way toward the ugliest of all bournes, success. I fly from that word as I do from styx, perfidy, the lust of money, and from those who pretend that they have been friends when they have been enemies. You have been my enemy, Charles, all the while that I was your friend. In your earliest days you could not bear to have me say something true before you had said it. I had warned you about that. It may be that there is genuine understanding of laws in what I write about the Indian. I do not know; but I think there is the same flagitious jealousy. We are always happening upon the same material, together or apart, the loadstone draws us.

The letter continues for several more pages. It climaxes in Dahlberg's last critique and words of advice to Olson:

Throw down your affectations, all those prissy verbalisms about being literary. The reason you want a literary relation with me is that you are furtive; you want only intimacy with some one who gives you big physiological ease; that's what everybody wants in this false polity. So long as there are no friendships, and people refuse to call love by the plain name that it is, we will be doomed as a nation, and our literature won't be worth more than that infamous poem of yours, or all that XYZ nonesense, or all that kind of congealed alphabet strutting. Go Back, I tell you, to your speculations, write about them as well as you can, never mind the people, or marx, or antimarx, use the books you have ransacked. You tell me I am not serious, are you droll? You damage your lines repeatedly because you want to be the vernacular clown or to be the jolly outhouse versifier, it gives you, you think, the common Touch. Ay, Touch, could you have but understood it, why you might have made some of my mistakes which appeared in that miscreant magazine, called Nimbus. Ay, Fox, did you get into that periodical?

My principal charge against you as a human being is that you are a self-lover, my complaint about you as a writer is that you deliberately refuse to find out what element is yours and to work in it.[29]

A few more letters passed between them. They were saddening, self-conscious attempts on both sides to fashion a common ground on which the friendship could be salvaged. Olson was quick to agree with one of Dahlberg's points: "Of course you and I often come to the same things and places, because I am also interested in beginnings. But I do not need to stress to you that there are several sorts of beginnings? And that the question of *origin* is as subtle as the morphological one?"[30] In the exchange of letters, Dahlberg once again refused the less personal and intense "terms" by which Olson hoped their relationship might be continued. Dahlberg would not countenance anything other than a complete friendship, in which the two of them worked intimately together and Olson continued to listen with deferential obedience to his master.

Olson was nonplused. His attempts at reconciliation only led him into a *cul de sac* because of Dahlberg's intransigence. He could remark, in the end, only on the "discrepancy" between their individual characters and, in exasperation, cry out against Dahlberg's use of the "gifts" he had given Olson as a kind of blackmail. "God damn you really," Olson exclaimed. "You make it such a shame that I ever accepted anything from you. Why do you have to do this, sad man? Why do you have to paw over everything until the other person can't even retain what they [sic] valued."[31] Reluctant to sign his name to the letter, Olson closed, as he had before, with the wish that Dahlberg had never saluted him "in praise of anything I did or was."

Dahlberg retaliated with his catalog of Olson's indebtedness to him. The wounds were deep and painful. Olson had taken advantage of him and his loneliness: "I had in my sorrow not a soul to turn to. You were poor, but you only relished my companionship when I could give you benefits, my table which was yours at any hour."[32] The final words were the most tortured:

Charles, do as you like. That is your life.... My relation with you, and how ill you guerdoned me for a heart plagued by your every mishap, that, Charles, is my hyssop and should I choose to drink the bitter herbs or water alone or with another, is my own portion and right.

As for a literary relationship with you, or anybody else, I prefer the passions of a Horatio for Hamlet than for some ice-cold and epicene epistles from a man who watched me suffer on the curbstones of New York, disavowed by the hacks of Grub Street and the diseased politicals; instead of honoring the man who had been his father by asking him to be his guest for a weekend now and then, he gave me for a hearth, a table and warmth, loving talk, a letter; ay, the letter killeth the spirit, and the friend.

Do I speak sense, or would you be so ridiculous as to call this ranting, or how, pray, does one say to you, I am hungry, feed me, I am alone, give me your hand, I am derided, do not pretend that this is an abstruse phrase. Yea, yea, I know a little about the heart, but enough that I can never know it; just enough to understand when it is open and when shut, when good and kind, when clandestine.

I sign my name as I always do in a rebuke, in love, in sorrow.[33]

In the face of this, Olson could only reassert his feelings of frustration. "To undo what you yourself don't do," he wrote in his last letter, "takes more than I've got to give. I don't like war between men. Or even believe in it. So please forgive me."[34]

CHAPTER SEVEN

Afterword: Conclusions

It was the quick Gaelic in Olson that drew me to him, but he was a good deal of the suety Swede, too, and that made him a sullen, water nature rather than fire and a Promethean liver. I did a portrait of him in the Flea of Sodom which is called Bellerophon. It is not a cruel or mean-hearted piece, dealing solely with the man who rides the horse to Parnassus with proud furies, imagining his iambic is any more than dust beseeching heaven for its alms. Besides, I wrote a little tribute in the book for him, but I could never content him. I have the highest feeling for friendship, and have never permitted the losses and the thistles that go with this sacred relationship to prevent me from trying again. If a man fails he is also at fault, and I cannot consider a single failure of mine that did not involve some flaw in my own character. It is said that the best cucumbers are grown at Antioch, the best lettuce at Smyrna, and the best rue at Myra, but where do we sow friendship? that and truth are the two marvelous perplexities in life. I deeply like Cicero's remark, "We are not born for ourselves alone."—DAHLBERG, in a letter to Dudley Nichols, April 20, 1953

Dahlberg's final scourging of Olson ended their friendship. Olson could not muster a reply, equal in invective, to parry this last attack. He no longer wished to engage Dahlberg on the level of past obligations, unfulfilled promises, accusations of betrayal and neglect, or the bonds of their intimate contacts over the years. The personal mythology of self which Dahlberg carefully nurtured and reinforced to shield him from "the world," as Olson experienced it, was impervious to Olson's attempts to fashion a more relaxed ground on which they both could meet and continue as friends.

With *The Flea of Sodom* Dahlberg had moved further into a position of intransigence—a preoccupation with the style and wisdom of the past—that could not accommodate Olson's activities and discoveries in the present. But it was not Olson so much as "the world," and especially the modern world, that Dahlberg rejected. Numerous critics have noted the withdrawal of Dahlberg into the past, his own and his culture's. Paul Carroll, for instance, remarked that Dahlberg "has worn the cloak of Diogenes with such conviction, day in and day out, decade after decade."[1] Alfred Kazin, reviewing *Because I Was Flesh* in 1961, observed:

106

Ever since the end of the 1930's, when Dahlberg withdrew from social realism by devouring the great scriptures and mythologies as if to inoculate himself against any danger from intellectual materialism in the future, he has made a point of dressing up his books with references to Ovid, Pliny, Luke, Jeremiah, Matthew, Mark, Sir Thomas Browne, Thoreau, and other sages. Dahlberg believes that the great writers can be therapists for those who suffer from invincible ignorance.[2]

Elsewhere in his review, Kazin puts his finger on the consuming personal concern that has marked Dahlberg's writing throughout—from the first novels to his autobiography thirty years later:

Dahlberg has gone back to his youth in Kansas City with a haunted, still unbelieving effort to master experiences to which all the rest of his life has been captive. After many years and many early tracings of the subject in his novels, Dahlberg still writes as if his prime need as a man and as a writer were to face his dispiriting memories. . . . Dahlberg takes his stand on fact: his life has been like no one else's. People's lives are not commensurable. Yet because of general deprivation in his youth, represented to his mind as a kind of cultural hunger, loneliness, cast-offness, Dahlberg wants to put his experiences with the world's—to list his experience among the great myths.[3]

As we have seen, as early as 1938, Dahlberg had had a sense of fatality about his own career, as when he wrote Waldo Frank that "the artist in America develops at his own peril. And so he finally writes himself into limbo."[4] It was this prophecy of isolation that Olson could not touch and would not partake of. It is intoned in *The Flea of Sodom* when Dahlberg declared: "I am . . . a solitary and loathe everyone, though I realize that as many owls and cormorants are in the wastes of spirit as in company."[5] Or when he scoffs at the world, ironically countering his opposition: "Be content, mockers, ruin enkindles my deity; and underneath my little rock of Peter sings the worm."[6] In Dahlberg the meaning of Keats' idea of "negative capability" has its full weight. The more reclusive, despondent, or pressed upon Dahlberg may have felt himself to be, the more fertile the ground for his creation because of this taxation of the spirit. Thus, Dahlberg breaks into song in the most unlikely circumstances: "For I sing in decayed places and have flayed my head for psalms and judgements that none will hear but the moles and the bats when the windows and lintels are rubbish."[7]

Around the time of his final falling-out with Olson, Dahlberg wrote to a friend upon the completion of *The Sorrows of Priapus*, a book about the carnal appetites of man and their eternally depressing consequences:

My own book is the result of the night I see about me, the killing of the filth and the May buds and the rale of the intellectual hermaphrodite.

I must work in the severest negatives, and though it may take a century before others may surmise that negations, too, are reaped in heaven and earth, and are not all life-hating, I speculate what man might be without a pudendum, seeing what he is with one. This is an exercise, too, in laughter and sorrow, and especially in self-knowledge. I see that I shall leave no land of the mind or the body unrecorded or untracked; let the poles wither me, and the straits rack me, if that be the inevitable journey to fate it cannot be an error. Others, coming later, replenishing their desert souls upon some page of mine, will then employ that compass that leads them to their own lodestar, their starry identity.[8]

It was perhaps inevitable that Dahlberg's writing moved more and more in the direction of the confessional. The figure of the Ishmael, which Olson helped to cast, focused attention on the self, almost to the entire exclusion of others. Olson sensed this tendency when he styled Dahlberg a monk. The results were books like *Because I Was Flesh* (1961), nominated for a National Book Award, that dealt primarily with the story of Dahlberg's mother, her tribulations and Dahlberg's poignant and finally transcendent embrace of her and all her faults. Or *The Confessions* (1971), where Dahlberg, like Tolstoy or St. Augustine, settled old scores, summed up his life, and once again condemned the modern world.

When I spoke with Dahlberg a few years before his death, he was working on still another volume of his "confessions," since the first installment took him only into the early 1940's. He continued to appear in print as an autobiographical writer in one of his last published works in *Prose* magazine, in a piece called "The Olive of Minerva," which dealt with his years as an expatriate on the Spanish island of Mallorca. In my interviews with him the subject had constantly been himself, his triumphs,—but mainly his defeats. These continued to trouble him throughout his last years.

After their reuniting with the publication of *Call Me Ishmael*, Olson began to have a sense of how he, too, was becoming a subject for Dahlberg's confessions. At first the realization brought irritation. Olson could not understand how Dahlberg could tell and retell the memories of their life together like the beads of a rosary. With *The Flea of Sodom*, though, Olson forgot his earlier anger and found much to praise in Dahlberg's autobiographical style:

> . . . you have personages, "I"'s, who fold the wisdom back into the vessel from which it came, it comes, you, the man, and therefore, give the truths an energy and place in which they express themselves, a meditation, an intercession. . . . It is a wonderful thing, Edward to do such INVOLU-TIONS now.[9]

But Olson's reservations remained:

> It is your "history" that bugs me, the suck of personages, events, images into your own vortex, where they swirl as ps., es., ism., of the micro-Ed, when Ed is there as "I"; but in the "revelations" the history goes off a piece and stays somewhere in between ED and—what?—It raises up the whole question, of how, what form forces all such things to their knees, makes them servant to that emporer—how, in fact, the god gets inside.[10]

Still, Olson could not refrain from leavening his critique with praise:

> It can be sd another way: you may remember the 1st piece of my work you saw. Anyhow, the curious thing is it has come up again in this way, in this opposition: the "heroic" vs the "ethic." One of the first reasons why your narratives are of first importance is, that you have broken the lyric "I" and the egotist "I" and the rational "I" completely. You have, therefore, made it possible for your own "I" to take on the force of the "Here". Thus ethic is disposed of—which has fed on the mediocrity of life as it is. You allow in (fr the Ixion wheel image, on) a multiple man (it is not so important as it may seem to those whom you know daily, and who know you, that it is Edward Dahlberg!).
>
> For such reason I should be tempted by the proposition to go too far, to say that the "ethic" steals back in, in the "revelations", because, by chiasma, that where Dahlberg is not folded in to this wonderful multiple "I" the Dahlberg whom we know, who knows us, is, by very loss of the myth-force, allowed in, and ethic comes with him![11]

Around the time that Olson was writing these comments to Dahlberg about the shifting personae of *The Flea of Sodom*, Olson himself was in the process of conceiving *The Maximus Poems,* a long sequence of poems that employed a variety of voices, which enabled Olson to move between the ancient history and mythology, the more recent history of Gloucester where the poems are "set," and the personal history of Olson himself. The main speaker in the poems is called Maximus—part legendary figure, part "objective" scholar/historian, part Olson. He is the presiding consciousness of the city, like Mr. Paterson in *Paterson*. Dahlberg's "multiple man" in *The Flea of Sodom* obviously struck Olson as being of important conceptual use in the poems he was planning. It allowed for the "multiple" interests that were propelling his imagination.

After the half year he spent in the Yucatan, Olson returned to Black Mountain College (where he continued to teach on a part time arrangement). He became the shaping force in the college's last years. As Martin Duberman writes in *Black Mountain: A Study in Community*: "the final desperate, illustrious years of the community are above all the story of Charles Olson's influence within it."[12] He goes on: "Charles Olson was unquestionably the heartbeat of Black Mountain during its last five years. . . . Olson dominated by the force of his personality. . . ."[13] That was no mean accomplishment, since the school housed personalities the likes of Paul Goodman, Merce Cunningham, John Cage, Franz Kline, Buckminster Fuller, and other dynamic artists and intellects. The atmosphere of the school, which need not be gone into at length here, was uniquely, intensely experimental and committed, though it often gave the impression of being chaotic, anarchistic, undisciplined. It was unlike any typical university, except for the seriousness of the intellectual demands it made on its students. Black Mountain proved to be just the right field for Olson to release his energies. Here Olson "emerged, 6 feet 7 inches, 250 pounds, and in his early forties, a mountain of tendentious energy, talking against anything that wasn't 'For use, now!'"[14]

Olson came to the fore in 1952 and remained a controlling influence until the college shut its doors in 1956. As a teacher he was of tremendous importance to the young writers who would get their starts at the college, among them Michael Ruhmacker, John Wieners, Joel Oppenheimer, Feilding Dawson, Ed Dorn, and Jonathan Williams. Duberman summarizes: "Along with the fact that most of those who came into prolonged contact with Olson ended up loving the man, I've been struck by a second fact: that even the most furious of his detractors single out important gains for themselves for having known him."[15]

Probably the most lasting impression, from a literary point of view, that Olson left on so many of the young writers at Black Mountain, on the Beats, and on the Post-Modernist poets in general was first articulate in Olson's early expression of his poetics in his "Projective Verse" essay of 1950. In the essay, Olson had taken an emphatic, impassioned stand about poetic composition, urging the use of an "OPEN" form of "COMPOSITION BY FIELD, as opposed to inherited line, stanza, over-all form, what is the 'old' base of the non-projective."[16] Olson was drawing on that other "tradition" of American poetry that extends from Whitman through William Carlos Williams and Ezra Pound and placing himself and his own work as the continuation of this line of non-academic, avant-garde poetry. Sherman Paul, in his *Olson's Push* asks the pertinent question:

> What then is new, not merely timely, in "Projective Verse"? Certainly not the insistence on the oral impulse, on open form, on presentation as against representation—or even the instruction in using the typewriter to score the poem. What is new, or made so by the way Olson appropriates and stresses it, is, in the words of "Human Universe," the insistence on repossessing man's dynamic. Projective verse is not only a poetics of presentation but a poetics of present experience, of enactment. It replaces

spectatorism with participation, and brings the whole self—the single intelligence: body, mind, soul—to the activity of creation. Dance, which Olson appreciated because it recalls us to our bodies and "we use ourselves," is a correlative of this poetics; and so are action painting and jazz, which poets at this time turned to because they offered the instruction they wanted. "There was no poetic," Olson says of this time. "It was Charlie Parker."

Charlie Parker reminds us that Olson more than any of his predecessors stresses breath. Both of the attentions he asks of poets in his formulation—

the HEAD, by way of the EAR, to the SYLLABLE
the HEART, by way of the BREATH, to the LINE

—involve the oral (aural) elements of verse. But Olson emphasizes the latter element because breath in determining the line not only shapes the poem but also "allows *all* speechforce of language back in." *Speech-force* translates "projective" into "projectile." The distinction he makes between ear and breath is a distinction between passive and active process, and it distinguishes Olson from Pound, whose "musical phrase," Olson notes, in considering field composition, was only a beginning.... But not Pound so much as Eliot is the poet against whom Olson makes his case. At the end of the essay, he concedes Eliot's speech-force but denies its projective quality; Eliot fails because "his root is the mind alone" and "in his listenings ... has stayed there where the ear and the mind are, has only gone from his fine ear outward rather than, as I say a projective poet will, down through the workings of his own throat to that place where breath comes from, where breath has its beginnings ... where, the coincidence is, all act springs."[17]

Dahlberg had been instrumental in helping Olson to define the process by which the projective poet should work; and Olson took Dahlberg's advice and constant proddings about the need to avoid delay and propel himself quickly, deeply, and personally into the work at hand—transforming these personal experiences into one of the general rules of Projective Verse composition:

Now (3) the *process* of the thing, how the principle can be made so to shape the energies that the form is accomplished. And I think it can be boiled down to one statement (first pounded into my head by Edward Dahlberg): ONE PERCEPTION MUST IMMEDIATELY AND DIRECTLY LEAD TO A FURTHER PERCEPTION. It means exactly what it says, is a matter of, at *all* points (even, I should say, of our management of daily reality as of the daily work) get on with it, keep moving, keep in, speed, the nerves, their speed, the perceptions, theirs, the acts, the split second acts, the whole business, keep it moving at fast as you can, citizen. And if you also set up as a poet, USE USE USE the process at all points, in any given poem always, always one perception must must must MOVE, INSTANTER, ON ANOTHER![18]

111

We see yet another aspect of what Olson had earlier learned from Dahlberg about the activity of writing come into play in a passage in Duberman's study where he briefly recreates one of Olson's writing classes and its general tenor. The emphasis on the personal, physical acts and facts of writing echo the encouragement of Dahlberg during Olson's apprenticeship:

> Olson used Dostoevski's *Notes from the Underground*, for example, to drive home the point that "there are certain things which you hide from close friends and admit only to yourself; the task of the writer is to dig out those things which you will not admit to yourselves." Olson did *not* mean thereby to encourage what he called "wretched lyricism," a sub-jectivism merely self-indulgent. Rather, he wanted his students to become "personal revolutionaries," to "more and more find the kinetics of experience disclosed—the kinetics of themselves as persons as well as of the stuff they have to work on, and by"; wanted, in short, "to release the person's energy word-wise, and thus begin the hammering of form out of content."[19]

Throughout his life, at Black Mountain, at The State University of New York at Buffalo, and at the University of Connecticut, Olson continued to have this significance as a teacher, this ability to affect those he was near. Thus, Robert Duncan introduced him before an address Olson gave at the University of California Poetry Conference at Berkeley in 1965: "I know when I'm coming home with a piece of colored glass that I've found that fits the design, and where to go for the fire at the center of things. For all of the poets who matter to me in my generation Charles Olson has been a Big Fire Source. One of the ones we have had to study."[20]

Perhaps what was so attractive about Olson, as a man and as a teacher and artist, was that he was interested in so much. The years until his death in 1970 were prolific. During this time he completed a long series of poems, *The Maximus Poems*, that stretches over three volumes. They contain Olson's voracious studies of ancient mythology and history, the history of Gloucester, and himself. There were many other works—poems, pamphlets, essays, reviews, stories—ranging from subjects as disparate as man during the Ice Ages to Shakespeare's metrics, from a pamphlet on the physical nature of poetry (*Proprioception*) to a list of readings (*A Bibliography on America for Ed Dorn*), from problems in topology to Bob Dylan. It is impossible to summarize Olson and his achievements as an artist except to say that he was, despite Dahlberg's injunction against being so, unique.

In the end, the influence of Dahlberg was incorporated into Olson's other expansive interests. Dahlberg's importance in Olson's early career surfaces, as we have seen, in several places, and at one time he referred to Dahlberg as "one of [his] chief intellectual disciplinarians."[21] There are the other allusions to Dahlberg's early nurturing of his creative talents in Ann Charters' *Olson/Melville*, and of course, there was the inscription to Dahlberg in *Call Me Ishmael*. But perhaps it is fair to say that Olson built on what Dahlberg had to teach him and then went his own way. He is alleged to have mentioned Dahlberg on his deathbed, with a chuckle. But he is also rumored to have called *Because I Was Flesh* "a filthy book" when the subject of Dahlberg came up in one of his seminars at Buffalo in the early sixties. Perhaps he simply "absorbed" Dahlberg, as Paul Metcalf claimed he did everyone close to him, using him to work in his behalf as "one of Charlie's troops."[22] Finally Olson's character is as mysterious as Dahlberg's, for neither lend themselves to simple explanations.

Dahlberg continued to live in New York City through the 1970's, the short confessional pieces and books emerging slowly, reflectively, bitterly. His enduring, inexhaustible theme was man's foolishness, as an individual and a species; and his style remained that of an Ecclesiastes who has wrestled with and tried to fathom the full absurdity of his age and himself and must proclaim that recognition, over and over again. *The Confessions*, for example, begin: "At Nineteen I was a stranger to myself. At forty I asked: Who am I? At fifty I concluded I would never know."[23] The book spins on from there in peroration:

> Know thyself is a wise Socratic exhortation, but how is it possible? Do I even understand a tithe of my nature? In truth, I know nothing about anybody, least of all about myself. No matter what I do it is likely to be wrong; one bungles everything, for the brain is feeble and an intuition is a saline and marshy guess. Whatever one has done he will do; that is his character, and he can neither improve nor escape it.[24]

The awareness of himself as an outsider, an Ishmael, persists:

> I have always been starved. Cloistered away in emaciated pariah rooms, I have sat in armchairs stuffed with the hemlock of wretched men who once occupied them, or tossed to and fro on old dry mattresses, dying from want of wool and love. It is plain that I have no choice. Could I compromise I would be more prudent and sensible. . . .
> It did not take me long in this life to realize that Job's muck-heap would be my throne and his shred my scepter. From the beginning I had all the qualifications for the occupation of author: obscurity, penury, and, I hoped, honesty, to which I could add ill hap, for he who is not enticed by the siren, misfortune, is a poltroon. I was never an opponent of the pittance one might receive from the world. What I would not do to get it was to be a sloven of Helicon. Why tell lies when one is going to die.[25]

113

Dahlberg was wounded by Olson's death. By the time *The Confessions* appeared, there was a chapter about him and their friendship. He spoke about their differences, about Olson's rejection of him, and concluded, philosophically, but with tenderness:

> It is not my purpose to resolve incomprehensible secrets of the flesh but to record them. Anyway, soon as a man left me or I him, and without any tincture of pride, I think I always was ready to allow him to go away. Is this self-love? I do not care for myself and I've never embraced that sorry creature. Could I be self-sufficient? It is true, we are as separated from others beneath the moon and the Pleiades as we are when we are covered with earth: I can see no real difference. This is involuntary; could I understand one human being I would know who commenced the universe.
> Olson had to renounce me. He had an ungovernable impulse to destroy himself. Is that bad? It was his inherent conviction. Why then judge him? Let me admit, it is absurd, but unless man is bizarre, he is not worth noticing. I shall always love Charles Olson and condemn him. Is that senseless? Then "smite me on the other cheek" is the demand of a great tragic Madman. Ordinary people will attribute this to self-killing. It is far deeper than that. It is the human way.[26]

In numerous, lengthy letters to me, Dahlberg recalled the events of his friendship with Olson, constantly asking me to "determine whether [he] was Charles' Iago or his Fool."[27] It is evident that he helped Olson enormously, and his loyalty to Olson was indisputable. But perhaps he attached an inordinate set of conditions to their friendship, to which Olson could not comply as completely as Dahlberg wished him to. I cannot judge between them, since both were passionate, headstrong individuals and their motivations are, finally, opaque. I would rather remember Dahlberg speaking fondly of Olson in his apartment in the fall of 1973, calling on one of those tranquil moments from the first summer of their friendship, in 1936, just a few weeks after they had met. He recalled how he marvelled as he watched Olson gracefully, powerfully swimming in the Atlantic off the coast of Gloucester, like some mythic figure about to come ashore and into his life.

114

NOTES

CHAPTER I

1 Edward Dahlberg letter to Alfred Stieglitz (August 12, 1936). The work alluded to is Lewis Mumford's *Herman Melville* (New York: Harcourt, Brace & Co., 1929). Dahlberg's letters to Stieglitz are in the Beinecke Rare Book and Manuscript Library at Yale University.

2 Charles John Olson, "The Growth of Herman Melville, Prose Writer and Poetic Thinker," Master's Thesis Wesleyan University 1933. The manuscript is in the Charles Olson Archives at the University of Connecticut Library, Storrs, Connecticut.

3 Conversation between John Cech and Edward Dahlberg (February 4, 1971).

4 Dahlberg letter to Harold Billings (November 19, 1967).

5 Dahlberg letter to Stieglitz. (See note #1 above.)

6 Conversation with Edward Dahlberg. (See note #3 above.)

7 Dahlberg letter to Stieglitz (August 23, 1936).

8 Unpublished Olson journal, n.p. In the Olson Archives.

9 Harold Billings, "Cabalist in the Wrong Season," in *Edward Dahlberg: American Ishmael of Letters*, ed. Harold Billings (Austin, Texas: Roger Beacham, 1968), p. 17.

10 Edward Dahlberg, "From Flushing to Calvary," *Contempo*, III (October 25, 1932). An essay about the novel. The section quoted here is reprinted in Jonathan Williams' "Edward Dahlberg's Book of Lazarus" in *American Ishmael of Letters*, op. cit., p. 30.

11 D. H. Lawrence, "Introduction" to *Bottom Dogs* (San Francisco: City Light Books, 1961), p. xvii.

12 Josephine Herbst, "Edward Dahlberg's *Because I Was Flesh*," in *American Ishmael of Letters*, p. 103.

13 Jonathan Williams, "Edward Dahlberg's Book of Lazarus," ibid. The brackets are mine.

14 Lawrence, op. cit., p. xiv.

15 Williams, pp. 29-30.

16 Dahlberg letter to Dudley Nichols (May 1, 1953). From the Collection of American Literature in the Beinecke Rare Book and Manuscript Library.

[17] Billings, "Cabalist," p. 16.

[18] Edward Dahlberg, *The Confessions of Edward Dahlberg* (New York: George Braziller, 1971), p. 291.

[19] "From Flushing to Calvary," *Contempo*, III. (See note #10 above.) This section is also reprinted by Williams, pp. 30-31.

[20] See Charles De Fanti's *The Wages of Expectation: A Biography of Edward Dahlberg* (New York: New York U. Press, 1979), pp. 1-25.

[21] Dahlberg recalled having gone to a screen-writing school in Hollywood and learned "the seven formulas" for film scripts. Though he wrote several, none were ever accepted for filming. Conversation with Dahlberg (October 19, 1973).

[22] Edward Dahlberg, "Ariel in Caliban," *This Quarter*, No. 4 (Monte Carlo, Spring 1929), pp. 228-36.

[23] See De Fanti, p. 108.

[24] Ibid., pp. 109-10.

[25] *Confessions*, op. cit., p. 251.

[26] Dahlberg letter to Waldo Frank (September 12, 1934). Dahlberg's correspondence with Frank is in the Special Collections of the University of Pennsylvania library, Philadelphia. The brackets are mine.

[27] Henry Hart, ed., *American Writers Congress* (New York, ca. 1935), p. 179. A pamphlet of their first proceedings.

[28] Dahlberg letter to Waldo Frank (February 24, 1935).

[29] *Confessions*, p. 286.

[30] Ibid., p. 263.

[31] Ibid., p. 293.

[32] Billings, "Cabalist," p. 16.

[33] *Confessions*, p. 262.

[34] *Epitaphs of Our Times: The Letters of Edward Dahlberg*, Edwin Seaver, ed. (New York, 1967), pp. 239-40.

[35] Herbst, op. cit., p. 104.

[36] Dahlberg letter to Stieglitz (July 27, 1936).

[37] Herbst, p. 96.

[38] Charles Olson, "The Post Office," an unpublished story, written ca. 1945, p. 24. In the Olson Archives. (See note #2 above.)

[39] *Classic Myths, The Classical High School Yearbook*, n.p. In the Olson Archives.

[40] Wilbert Snow, "A Teacher's View," in "A gathering for Charles Olson," pp. 40-41. The pamphlet is a transcription of "part of a Memorial Program for Charles Olson ... given at the Honors College, Wesleyan Uni-

versity, Middleton, Connecticut, on Wednesday, November 18, 1970" and first appeared in the *Massachusetts Review*, XII, No. 1 (Winter 1971), pp. 33-57.

[41] Ibid., p. 42.

[42] "The Growth of Herman Melville," p. 90. (See note #2 above.)

[43] See Ann Charters, *Olson/Melville: A Study in Affinities* (Oyez Press: Berkeley, 1968) for a more complete discussion of the circumstances of Olson's location of the Melville library.

[44] Charles Olson, *Call Me Ishmael* (New York: Reynal and Hitchcock, 1947), p. 16.

[45] "The Post Office," op. cit., pp. 32-33. The abbreviations are Olson's.

[46] Charles Olson, 'Journal of Swordfishing Cruise on the Doris M. Hawes... July 1936," in *Olson: The Journal of the Charles Olson Archives* (Storrs, Connecticut: U. of Connecticut Library) No. 7, Spring 1977, p. 28.

[47] *Maps #4: Special Charles Olson Issue*, ed. George Butterick (Shippens-burg, Pa., 1971), p. 44.

CHAPTER II

[1] Unpublished notes (ca. 1938-1940). In the Olson Archives. The abbreviations are Olson's.

[2] Dahlberg postcard to Olson (September 14, 1936). In the Olson Archives.

[3] Edward Dahlberg, "Preface" to *Bottom Dogs* (San Francisco: City Lights Books, 1961). When the novel was re-issued, Dahlberg insisted on a preface to counter Lawrence's "Introduction" and to confess what he felt were the flaws of the novel.

[4] Dahlberg letter to Olson (August 3, 1948).

[5] The dismissal is explained by Henry G. Alsberg, a later director of the Federal Writer's Project in a letter to Waldo Frank (December 16, 1938). The letter is in the Waldo Frank Collection of the Rare Book and Manu-script Library of the University of Pennsylvania in Philadelphia.

[6] Edward Dahlberg, *Do These Bones Live* (New York: Harcourt Brace, 1941), p. 25. Hereafter abbreviated as *Bones* in these notes.

[7] Ibid., p. 21.

[8] Dahlberg letter to Dorothy Norman (December 14, 1937). In the holdings of the Beinecke Rare Book and Manuscript Library at Yale.

[9] Ibid. (July 6, 1937).

[10] Dahlberg, *Confessions*, p. 296.

[11] Dahlberg, *Bones*, p. 28.

[12] The inscription is found in Olson's copy of *From Flushing to Calvary* in the Olson Archives.

¹³ Edward Dahlberg, "My Friends Stieglitz, Anderson and Dreiser" in *Alms for Oblivion: Essays by Edward Dahlberg* (Minneapolis: University of Minnesota Press, 1964), p. 12.

¹⁴ Dahlberg letter to Dorothy Norman (September 13, 1937).

¹⁵ Dahlberg letter to John Cech (January 27, 1972).

¹⁶ Dahlberg letter to Olson (January 31, 1937).

¹⁷ "Facts," unpublished notes in the Olson Archives. Olson made a copy of his answers to "Civil Service Questionnaire, form #57" dated August 11, 1942.

¹⁸ Paul Metcalf in an address at the University of Connecticut Library Arts Festival (April, 1973).

¹⁹ John Finch, "Dancer and Clerk" in "A Gathering for Charles Olson," p. 39. (See note #38 for Chapter I.)

²⁰ See Dorothy Norman's "An American Place" in *America and Alfred Stieglitz*, ed. Dorothy Norman, Waldo Frank, Lewis Mumford, et al. (New York, 1934), pp. 126-51.

²¹ Dahlberg postcard to Waldo Frank (December 30, 1936).

²² Dahlberg letter to Waldo Frank (January 4, 1937).

²³ In conversation with Mrs. Norman (November 17, 1973).

²⁴ Ibid.

²⁵ William Wasserstrom, ed., *Civil Liberties and the Arts* (Ithaca, New York: Cornell University Press, n.d.), p. xvii.

²⁶ Ann Charters, *Olson/Melville*, p. 5. (See note #41 for Chapter I.)

²⁷ Dahlberg letter to Olson (October 27, 1937).

²⁸ Dahlberg letter to Dorothy Norman (August 25, 1937).

²⁹ Olson letter to Dorothy Norman ("Cambridge (March)" /1938/).

³⁰ "Facts," p. 2. (See note #17 above.)

³¹ Olson's Graduate School Records, in the Harvard Archives. Used by special permission of the Registrar, Harvard University.

³² Dahlberg letter to Olson (December 2, 1937).

³³ Ibid. (December 13, 1937.)

³⁴ Olson letter to Dorothy Norman (ca. January 1938).

³⁵ Wilbert Snow, "A Teacher's View," op. cit., p. 41.

³⁶ Dahlberg letter to Olson (January 21, 1937).

³⁷ Dahlberg letter to Dorothy Norman (June 24, 1938).

³⁸ *Confessions*, p. 281.

³⁹ Dahlberg letter to Cech (January 20, 1971).

[40] Olson letter to Dahlberg (May 9, 1947).

[41] Dahlberg letter to Cech (January 27, 1972).

[42] Dahlberg letter to Olson (February 9, 1938).

[43] Dahlberg letter to Dorothy Norman (February 36, 1938).

[44] Olson letter to Dorothy Norman (March '38).

[45] Dahlberg letter to Cech (January 20, 1971).

[46] Dahlberg letter to Dorothy Norman (June 30, 1938).

[47] Olson letter to Dorothy Norman (July 27, 1938).

[48] Ibid. (August 14, 1938).

[49] According to Harold Billings, Dahlberg's friend, bibliographer, and the curator of his papers at the University of Texas, Dahlberg often wrote and completely reworked his essays over a period of years until he was satisfied with them.

[50] Olson letter to Dorothy Norman (August 14, 1938).

[51] Dahlberg letter to Dorothy Norman (August 14, 1938).

[52] Olson letter to Dorothy Norman ("Friday Night," n.d. [ca. September 1938]).

[53] Ibid. ("Sunday night!", n.d. [September 1938]).

[54] Dahlberg letter to Dorothy Norman (September 7, 1938).

[55] *Bones*, p. 40.

[56] Dahlberg letter to Dorothy Norman (September 16, 1938).

[57] Ibid.

[58] In a letter to the poet, Robert Creeley in 1951, Olson alludes to the mayhem of these last days of work on the essay: "like writing—wrote 1st piece, Lear—MD, 72 hrs straight, and two quarts of Vat 69 (then). No food. Nothing. Talkin to myself." In the Olson Archives.

[59] Charles Olson, "Lear and Moby-Dick," *Twice-A-Year*, Fall, 1938, p. 165.

[60] Ibid., p. 168.

[61] Ibid., pp. 171-72.

[62] Ibid., p. 187.

[63] Ibid., p. 188.

[64] Ibid., p. 189.

[65] Dahlberg letter to Stieglitz (September 19, 1938).

[66] In conversation with Dorothy Norman (November 17, 1973).

[67] Dahlberg letter to Stieglitz (October 9, 1938).

[68] Ibid.

[69] Ibid. (September 29, 1938).

[70] Ibid. (November 3, 1938).

CHAPTER III

[1] Dahlberg, *Confessions*, p. 259.

[2] Olson letter to Dahlberg (April 18, 1949).

[3] From Olson's notes for his "Application for Federal Employment," May 9, 1944. Unpublished notes in the Olson Archives.

[4] Dahlberg letter to Stieglitz (November 21, 1938).

[5] "Fact Sheet." (See note #17 for Chapter II.)

[6] Olson letter to Dorothy Norman (January 15, 1939).

[7] Dahlberg letter to Cech (January 15, 1939).

[8] Dahlberg letter to Stieglitz (December 30, 1938).

[9] Ibid. (November 7, 1938).

[10] Ibid. (December 30, 1938).

[11] Olson letter to Dorothy Norman ("October" [1938]).

[12] Ibid.

[13] Ibid.

[14] Unpublished notebook, "Summer & Fall, 1939." This entry is dated October 20, 1939. In the Olson Archives.

[15] Olson letter to Dorothy Norman (August 18, 1940).

[16] *Bones*, op. cit., p. 40.

[17] "Dostoevsky and The Possessed," *Twice-A-Year*, No. 5-6 (Fall-Winter 1940), p. 232.

[18] Ibid., p. 236. The reference here is to Revelations, 3:16-18.

[19] Ibid., pp. 236-37. There is also the echo of the title to Dahlberg's third novel, *Those Who Perish*, in the passage.

[20] Ibid., p. 237.

[21] Dahlberg letter to Olson (May 17, 1947).

[22] Ibid.

[23] "Lear and Moby-Dick," op. cit., p. 172.

[24] Dahlberg letter to Dorothy Norman (June 13, 1938).

[25] Dahlberg letter to Olson (July 18, 1940). The capitalization and spelling appears as it does in the letter.

[26] "Dostoevsky and The Possessed," p. 231.

[27] Unpublished notebook in the Olson Archives ("begun Sept. 1, 1936), n.p.

[28] Olson letter to Dorothy Norman (August 14, 1938).

[29] *Bones*, pp. 19-20.

[30] Ibid., p. 69.

[31] Ibid., p. 40.

[32] Ibid., p. 42.

[33] Dahlberg letter to Olson (July 18, 1940). The spelling is Dahlberg's.

[34] Ibid.

[35] Charters, op. cit., p. 5.

[36] Olson letter to Dorothy Norman (July 30, 1940).

[37] Ibid. (August 18, 1940).

[38] Olson letter to Waldo Frank (ca. December 1939).

[39] Charters, p. 9.

[40] Ibid.

[41] Dahlberg letter to Stieglitz (May 3, 1944).

[42] Unpublished manuscript in the Olson Archives.

CHAPTER IV

[1] Telephone conversation with John Cech (October 11, 1973).

[2] Interview with Dahlberg (February 8, 1971).

[3] Dahlberg letters to Olson (April 25, 1947).

[4] Ibid.

[5] Dahlberg letter to John Cech (October 20, 1971).

[6] Dahlberg letter to John Cech (October 20, 1971).

[7] *Confessions*, p. 259.

[8] Ibid.

[9] Ibid.

[10] Ibid., p. 261.

[11] Ibid.

[12] Interview with Dahlberg (October 19, 1973).

[13] *Bones*, p. 37.

[14] Dahlberg letter to Olson (August 3, 1948).

[15] Dahlberg letter to Olson (April 17, 1947).

[16] *Bones*, p. 34.

[17] Unpublished loose manuscript notes (ca. 1939-1940). In the Olson Archives.

[18] Unpublished Notebook in the Olson Archives, "Summer & Fall, 1929." This entry is dated October 20, 1939.

[19] See note #17.

[20] "In Adullam's Lair," an unpublished manuscript in the Olson Archives. The manuscript may have been written around 1939 and have been a chapter of the Melville study Olson showed to Dahlberg.

[21] *Call Me Ishmael*, p. 100.

[22] Waldo Frank.

[23] Unpublished, undated and unnumbered manuscript notes. (ca. 1938 or 1939) in the Olson Archives. The underlinings are Olson's.

[24] *Bones*, pp. 70-71.

[25] Interview with Dahlberg (February 8, 1971).

[26] "In Adullam's Lair," op. cit.

[27] *Bones*, p. 109.

[28] Ibid., p. 104.

[29] Dahlberg telephone conversation with Cech (October 14, 1973).

[30] See note #17.

[31] Unpublished notebook in the Olson Archives ("Summer & Fall, 1939"). This particular entry is undated.

[32] "The Kingfishers" in *Archeologist of Morning: The Collected Poems Outside the Maximus Series* (London: Cape Goliard Press, 1940), n.p.

[33] Unpublished notes in the Olson Archives (ca. 1939-1940).

[34] Dahlberg letter to Cech (January 27, 1972).

CHAPTER V

[1] Alfred Kazin's review appeared in *Books*, April 13, 1941.

[2] Mary M. Colum's review appeared in *American Mercury*, June 1941.

[3] *Bones*, op. cit., pp. 84-85.

[4] Both William Carlos Williams' *In The American Grain* (1925) and D. H. Lawrence's *Studies in Classic Literature* (1923) figure as prominent progenitors of *Do These Bones Live*. Dahlberg refers to both in his book and draws heavily on the themes Williams and Lawrence explored in their works. Chief among these was the sterilizing effects Puritanism had had on American writers. Another essay could be written on the relationships between these three works and, later, Olson's *Call Me Ishmael*.

[5] *Bones*, p. 77.

[6] By Harold Billings' estimate, it sold less than 375 from the original edition. See "Cabalist in the Wrong Season," op. cit., p. 18.

[7] Williams letter to Louis Untermeyer (14 March 1941), quoted in Mike Weaver, *William Carlos Williams: The American Background* (New York, 1971), p. 204.

[8] See Jules Chametzy's "Edward Dahlberg, Early and Late"; Herbert Miller's "Do These Bones Live"; and Kay Boyle's "A Man in the Wilderness" —all collected in *Edward Dahlberg: A Tribute*, ed. Jonathan Williams (New York: David Lewis, Inc., 1970). Also see Alfred Kazin's "The Eloquence of Failure"; Robert Kindrick's "The Benevolent Scourge: Edward Dahlberg and Modern American Letters"; and Paul Carroll's "An Introduction to Edward Dahlberg"—collected in *American Ishmael of Letters*, ed. Harold Billings (Austin, Texas: Roger Beacham, 1968).

[9] Dahlberg letter to Olson (April 9, 1947).

[10] Phil Casey, "Writing What He Must, Getting By—But Barely," *The Washington Post* (Monday, June 18, 1973), p. B1.

[11] Paul Carroll, "An Introduction to Edward Dahlberg," in *The Edward Dahlberg Reader*, ed. Paul Carroll (New York: New Directions, 1967), p. xii.

[12] Dahlberg letter to Olson (April 9, 1947).

[13] Dahlberg letter to Alfred Stieglitz (October 24, 1941).

[14] Ibid. (October 20, 1943).

[15] Ibid. (August 11, 1944).

[16] Ibid. (April 26, 1944).

[17] Ibid. (May 24, 1944).

[18] Conversation with Dahlberg (February 1, 1971).

[19] Dahlberg letter to Stieglitz (May 18, 1946).

[20] Dahlberg letter to Olson (April 9, 1947).

[21] Olson letter to Dahlberg (n.d.).

[22] Dahlberg letter to Olson (April 17, 1947). "The Noah, the Christ, and the Moses" refer to chapter titles in *Call Me Ishmael*.

[23] Ibid. (May 2, 1947).

[24] Ibid. (April 25, 1947).

[25] Ibid. (June 9, 1947).

[26] Ibid. (April 25, 1947).

[27] Olson letter to Dahlberg (April 23, 1947).

[28] Ibid.

[29] Dahlberg letter to Olson (April 25, 1947).

[30] Ibid.

[31] Ibid.

[32] Olson letter to Dahlberg (April 29, 1947).

[33] Ibid.

[34] Dahlberg letter to Olson (May 2, 1947).

35 Ibid.

36 Olson letter to Dahlberg (May 9, 1947). The first chapter of *Do These Bones Live* was titled "The Man-Eating Fable." In the chapter Dahlberg characterized the great literature of the past that compelled him as taking up the capacity of man to devour other men, metaphorically or literally: "Hamlet, Macbeth, Timon, these are our fables, aye, the proverbs, the Golgothas we have memorized, but history, the ACT, is the sign of Cain. Terror is the lodestar, and its mark is in the first blood-besmeared pictures in the Paleolithic caves, in human sacrifice, in murder and war. Shakespeare and Goya forced men to cringe before thwir own dark beast abysses; we cower as we look at Goya's SATURN DEVOURING HIS SON or at his painting of the officer measuring with carnivore satisfaction the simple soldier hanging from a tree,—as we hear Timon's ultimate blasphemy: 'Nor on the beasts themselves, the birds and fishes; you must eat men.' These are the tragical MOUSE-TRAP paintings and plays to bait the conscience of men" (p. 6). The spelling in the letter is Olson's.

37 "Answers to Civil Service questions: form #57." (See note #3 for Chapter III.)

38 Charters, *Olson/Melville*, p. 9.

39 Charters, p. 9. The quote is from an Olson letter to Charters (February 14, 1968).

40 *Call Me Ishmael*, op. cit., p. 71.

41 Ibid., p. 96.

42 "Baptized in the Name of the Devil," *New York Times Book Review*, April 6, 1947, p. 14.

43 *Call Me Ishmael*, pp. 99-100.

44 Ibid., pp. 118-19.

45 Dahlberg letter to Olson (April 21, 1947).

46 Ibid. (May 17, 1947). Dahlberg later attacked Williams in more length in "Word-Sick and Place-Crazy" in *Alms for Oblivion* (Minneapolis: University of Minnesota Press, 1964), pp. 20-27.

47 From an unpublished manuscript on Ezra Pound in the Olson Archives. The section is marked "First Canto, January 5, 1946," n.p.

48 Unpublished notebook in the Olson Archives, "Washington Spring 1945." The underscorings and ellipses are Olson's.

49 Ibid.

50 Unpublished, loose manuscript note in the Olson Archives (ca. winter 1945).

51 "Projective Verse," collected in *Human Universe and Other Essays* by Olson, ed. Donald Allen (New York: New Directions, 1967), pp. 52-53.

[52] The inscription is in Dahlberg's copy of *Call Me Ishmael* at the Academic Center, University of Texas Library, Austin, Texas. It is dated, "Washington 1948."

CHAPTER VI

[1] *The Flea of Sodom* (London: Peter Nevill Ltd., 1950), pp. 17-18. Hereafter abbreviated as *The Flea.*

[2] Dahlberg letter to Olson (August 3, 1948).

[3] Olson letter to Dahlberg (September 20, 1948).

[4] *The Flea*, pp. 78-79.

[5] *The Maximus Poems* (New York: Corinth Press, 1960), p. 35.

[6] *The Flea*, pp. 64-65.

[7] Dahlberg letter to Dudley Nichols (March 31, 1953). In the American Literature holdings of the Bienecke Rare Book and Manuscript Library, Yale University.

[8] Dahlberg letter to Olson (ca. November-December 1948). The capitalization is Dahlberg's.

[9] Ibid. (January 18, 1949).

[10] *The Flea*, p. 113.

[11] Ibid., p. 113.

[12] See Martin Duberman's account of Dahlberg's coming and going in *Black Mountain: An Exploration in Community* (New York, 1973), pp. 319-22.

[13] Olson letter to Dahlberg (August 29, 1950).

[14] Ibid.

[15] Olson letter to Dahlberg (September 29, 1950). Olson is here referring to the written endorsement Dahlberg gave *Call Me Ishmael* when it was reprinted by New Directions in 1950. The spelling is Olson's.

[16] Ibid.

[17] Ibid.

[18] Ibid. (November 16, 1950). The spelling and spacing is Olson's.

[19] "Laurels for Borrowers," *Freeman*, II (December 17, 1951), pp. 187-90.

[20] Olson letter to Dahlberg (December 19, 1951).

[21] Dahlberg letter to Olson (December 31, 1951). The conflict with Van Doren was a result of the reviews Dahlberg was doing for *The Freeman.*

[22] Olson letter to Dahlberg (January 22, /1952/). The spelling is Olson's.

[23] Dahlberg letter to Olson (August 20, 1955).

[24] Ibid. *The Freeman* was a right-wing magazine, published by John Chamberlain, whom Dahlberg had known in the thirties when they were both involved in the Communist movement. Like Dahlberg, Chamberlain had reacted against the ideology of the Left. The first issue of the magazine came out in 1950, at the beginning of the MacCarthy furor, and it ceased publication in 1953. Dahlberg seems to be implying that he disliked the politics of the Right as much as those of the Left.

[25] Olson letter to Dahlberg (November 12, 1955). The spelling, orthography, and punctuation are Olson's.

[26] Ibid.

[27] Ibid.

[28] Dahlberg letter to Olson (November 16, 1955). The poem Dahlberg is referring to here is "O'Ryan 2." The beginning of the poem and the lines Dahlberg found objectionable read:

> Tell me something, tell me
> how you got that way
>
> how'dya lose your
> what stuck you in the pants
>
> why did they ask you
> to take on so much
>
> Tell me something, tell me
> what made you do it
>
> why did you buy
> so much shit
>
> how come you got so far off
> the rail

The poem is reprinted in *Archeologist of Morning: The Collected Poems* outside the Maximus Series (London: Cape Goliard Press, 1970), n.p.

[29] Dahlberg letter to Olson (November 16, 1955).

[30] Olson letter to Dahlberg (November 18, 1955).

[31] Ibid.

[32] Dahlberg letter to Olson (November 24, 1955).

[33] Ibid.

[34] Olson letter to Dahlberg (October 19, 1955).

CHAPTER VII

[1] Paul Carroll, "An Introduction to Edward Dahlberg," in *The Edward Dahlberg Reader*, ed. Paul Carroll (New York: New Directions, 1967), p. xviii.

[2] Alfred Kazin, "The Eloquence of Failure," collected in *An American Ishmael of Letters*, op. cit., p. 114.

[3] Ibid., p. 112.

[4] Dahlberg letter to Waldo Frank (November 7, 1938).

[5] *The Flea of Sodom*, p. 19.

[6] Ibid., p. 21.

[7] Ibid., p. 48.

[8] Dahlberg letter to Dudley Nichols (May 4, 1953).

[9] Olson letter to Dahlberg ("tuesday july august 2 50"). The spelling and orthography are Olson's.

[10] Ibid. ("Monday Aug 29 50").

[11] Ibid.

[12] Martin Duberman, *Black Mountain: An Exploration in Community* (New York: Anchor Books, 1973), p. 338.

[13] Ibid., p. 356.

[14] Ibid., p. 354.

[15] Ibid., p. 392.

[16] "Projective Verse," p. 52.

[17] Sherman Paul, *Olson's Push: Origin, Black Mountain and Recent American Poetry* (Baton Rouge: Louisiana State University Press, 1978), pp. 39-40.

[18] "Projective Verse," pp. 52-53.

[19] Duberman, p. 393.

[20] Charles Olson, *Causal Mythology*, a transcription of "A lecture delivered to the University of California Poetry Conference, July 20, 1965, at Berkeley," ed. Donald Allen (San Francisco: Four Seasons Foundation, 1969), p. 1.

[21] Olson's biographical entry in Stanley J. Kunitz's *Twentieth Century Authors: First Supplement* (New York: The H. W. Wilson Company, 1963), p. 741.

[22] Paul Metcalf in an address at the University of Connecticut Library Arts Festival, April 1973.

[23] *The Confessions of Edward Dahlberg*, op. cit., p. 3.

[24] Ibid.

[25] Ibid., pp. 6-7.

[26] Ibid., p. 261.

[27] Dahlberg letter to Cech (January 27, 1972).

www.ingramcontent.com/pod-product-compliance
Lightning Source LLC
Chambersburg PA
CBHW061831040426
42447CB00012B/2914